Footloose and Financially Free

Footloose AND Financially Free

A guide to thinking *and* feeling *your way to* success

Julie Macken

milli naire

First published in Australia in 2010 by Macmillionaire
PO Box 3888, Mosman 2088 Australia
www.macmillionaire.com
copyright © 2010, Julie Macken

All rights reserved. No part of this publication may be reproduced, stored in a retrieval system, or transmitted, in any form or by any means, without the prior written permission of the publisher, nor be otherwise circulated in any form of binding or cover other than that in which it was published and without a similar condition being imposed on the subsequent purchaser.

The author recommends that before making financial decisions readers satisfy themselves independently as to the relevance of the material in this book to their own particular circumstances. It is the intent of the author to offer information of a general nature to assist individuals in their quest for happiness and prosperity. In the event that you use any of the information in this book, the author and the publisher take no responsibility for your actions.

National Library of Australia Cataloguing-in-Publication entry

Author:	Macken, Julie.
Title:	Footloose and financially free: a guide to thinking and feeling your way to success/Julie Macken.
ISBN:	9780980760903 (pbk.)
Subjects:	Success—Psychological aspects. Finance, Personal.

Dewey Number: 158.1

Distribution in Australia and New Zealand: Dennis Jones & Associates, Unit 1, 10 Melrich Road, Bayswater, Victoria 3153
www.dennisjones.com.au
Project management and design: Best Legenz www.bestlegenz.com.au
Printed in China by Bookbuilders

Contents

Before you begin		v
1	**Freedom to choose**	1
	Expand your mind and improve your life	
2	**Innocently imaginative**	7
	Stimulating the imagination you were born with	
3	**Invincibility of the mind**	19
	Developing resilient thinking	
4	**Incurably optimistic**	35
	Adopting a buoyant attitude	
5	**Lucky links**	47
	Becoming aware of the potential in those around you	
6	**Reinvention**	59
	Creating a new identity for yourself	
7	**Serendipity**	71
	Listening to your inner voice and honing your instincts	
8	**Pursuing diversity**	81
	Taking chances and chasing opportunity	
9	**Embracing new possibilities**	91
	Allowing your mind to be open to new expectations	
10	**The launching pad**	97
	Designing your own destiny before someone else does it for you	
11	**Hidden potential**	109
	Extending your awareness of the potential of the people and places that surround you	
12	**Perfect world**	121
	Enhancing your ability to see your world the way you want it to be	

13	**Powerful partnerships**	135
	Bringing out the strength in others so they shine on your parade	
14	**Running past the finishing line**	147
	Balancing work and play and remembering to have fun	
15	**Magnificent Mentors**	157
	Learning and being inspired by other's brilliance	
16	**The rules of the money game**	169
	Building the confidence to make decisions	
17	**Emotional buoyancy**	179
	Developing faith in yourself	
18	**Manoeuvrability of the mind**	185
	Directing your thoughts along a positive stream	
19	**The X factor of human achievement**	195
20	**Funancial freedom**	201
	Making the most of your multi-faceted mind	
21	**Renovate your life**	211
	Managing ongoing personal expansion	
22	**Make your life an adventure**	217
	Embracing all that you can be	
About the author		226
Acknowledgements		228

Before you begin

Although I achieved Financial Freedom in just fourteen months, the stories herein begin from my early childhood. The reason for this will become clear as you progress. Before I began writing, I wondered where to start because I felt that so many messages were of value. I wanted to put them all in the first chapter. Thankfully, a fellow writer suggested I relax and write random stories and then intuitively find a natural order. Following his advice paid off and I was able to order the concepts in a logical sequence.

But this still left the challenge of presenting complex material in a simple, easy-to-understand format and, for this reason, you may find that a subject is touched upon that you feel warrants further examples or clarification. I encourage you to continue reading for two reasons; the first being that many of the concepts are given greater detail and a broader perspective in subsequent chapters; the second reason relates to our ability to store information that we do not yet understand or do not yet have a use for, yet instinctively know will be of use to us at some future point. An example of this is when I first read Napolean Hill's *Think and Grow Rich*. I loved the book but didn't understand some of it. The messages within were somehow elusive yet I found the book had a strangely hypnotic effect on me. I trusted that the material presented would eventually hold greater meaning for me. In the months that followed, my intuitive response paid off. I had numerous profound experiences; moments when one of the concepts suddenly had clear meaning and relevance.

There are many beliefs and opinions surrounding the subjects of wealth and happiness. Some believe that having more money will bring more happiness into their life but having more money simply brings more choices into your life. And life is not about getting happy and staying there. It's about finding happiness again and again and continually discovering new reasons to be happy.

Many individuals attribute their destiny to something outside of themself which results in a perception of restriction or lack of control. This book is all about ***you*** accessing and radiating your personal power by developing a fuller appreciation of your freedom of choice. Even when you think your choices of action are limited, this book will help you to remember that your choices of thought are vast and our thoughts are the precursors of our action. The freedom we all seek lies in our ability to focus and control the direction of our thoughts while being guided by our emotions.

Freedom to choose

Expand your mind and improve your life

It is our choices, Harry, that show what we truly are, far more than our abilities.
From *Harry Potter and the Chamber of Secrets* by JK Rowling

If someone had told me when I left school that I would one day become wealthy by using a creative approach to making money, I would have laughed. For years I didn't think I had a creative bone in my body. If you're worried that you are not the creative type, *relax*. This book is designed to stimulate the imagination you were born with. It will help you to expand your mind and your heart so that you can enjoy more happiness, more fun, better relationships and more money.

Put to the test

My palms were sweating and my heart was pounding. Looking around, I noticed many of my classmates looked as nervous as I felt. With pale faces and rigid expressions we filed into the school hall. The moment of truth had arrived ... our final high school maths exam.

Examination time seemed like an ugly ending to school life. The results of these exams had the potential to make or break a career aspiration. Failing any one exam meant you were ineligible for university. The only way you could re-sit an exam was to attend an extra year of high school and sit all the exams again.

Maths had been my biggest challenge, so it was the exam I dreaded most. The subject had always been a struggle and extra tuition hadn't seemed to help much. But I had persevered because I'd been told it would be useful in the outside world. Most of the examination questions were beyond me so I sat feeling clueless, glancing at the clock.

Finally, when our time was up, I felt unexpected relief wash over me. It wasn't that I thought that I'd done well. On the contrary, I suspected that I had failed miserably. I was just incredibly glad it was over so that, regardless of the result, I could get on with my next priority: to celebrate that this torturous competition was finally over.

When the results came out, I discovered that not only had I failed maths but so had most of my classmates. It didn't make me feel much better. Failing didn't feel good; it felt too final. But flunking maths was not a big surprise because I didn't like it and didn't expect to do well. The real shock came when I discovered that I'd also failed economics and dropped a level in English. I was really disappointed because I liked both these subjects. I admired my economics teacher because she was intelligent and engaging. I found her lessons interesting and the subject matter was different to anything else I had studied. Concepts like supply and demand and marginal utility intrigued me, as they had a place in my mind in what I perceived as the real world outside school.

Many of my friends went on to university. But with two outright failures I left school believing I was pretty dumb. Some friends reassured me, saying it didn't matter that I wasn't very smart because I was fun to be with. And for quite a number of years I believed that being fun was all I was good for.

Pressure to conform

Believing that success was the result of hard work and academic achievement, I left school thinking that becoming a high achiever or amassing a fortune was too far out of reach for a girl like me. Maybe I was lazy but the thought of hard work made me want to run and hide. I had always found study a chore so it was a relief knowing that I would not have to face years of swotting at university.

As a teenager, I failed to conform to the stereotype student presented by society and as an adult I persevered for years thinking that I had to "fit in" with what others felt comfortable with. Yet it turned out that I did not need a university degree to become successful. I simply became very good at being me. The more I ignored pressure to conform, the more comfortable I became with myself and the easier it was for me to discover my real strengths.

A string of stories

In the chapters that follow I reveal my learning curves. The ideas I present are intended to help you to shine and become very good at being you. A message that is repeated throughout is how important it is to be clear about what you want. Sounds so simple but our focus gets blurred by the contrast we perceive in our constantly changing horizons.

Our lives are like a string of stories that spring from our constant yearning for validation. Yet in seeking approval from others we can fall into the trap of forgetting that our best source of validation comes from within and it comes in the form of positive emotion.

Our life stories are of events that stir our emotions and they reflect where our choices have led us and who they have caused us to become. As you read, consider your own stories, dreams and learning curves and allow my words to spark your imagination and activate your sixth sense.

The knack of achieving great results with seemingly little effort dawned on me as I learned to tune in to my inner guidance. I had previously reasoned my way through life, thinking that intuition was a talent that few were born with. Now I understand that it is available to us all and my aim is not to teach you *what to do* but to inspire you to *think for yourself* and to tune in to your own inner guidance.

Expand your mind and improve your life

I used to wonder, *is it greedy to want to have it all? Would people think less of me if I had money* and *happiness?* Contrary to what some believe, there is an abundance of wonderful things in our world and your having more money won't mean someone else will go without. A common misconception about money is that there is only so much to go around. When people approach money with this attitude it is bound to conjure up negative emotion. It leads people to think that money is hard to obtain or that they have to compete with others because it is in limited supply.

Although I left school thinking I wasn't very smart, I eventually discovered that I was neither lazy nor stupid. When I found things that I felt passionate about I realised that I was more clever than I thought and I became more motivated to work towards things I wanted. And when I took a more creative approach to making money, I removed the pressure of feeling that I had to compete with others.

When I learned to think more expansively, I discovered that I could easily increase my levels of happiness and prosperity. Today, I have much more to offer the world and those around me than when I was clueless and uncertain. Now I use my imagination to see the endless choices available to me, whereas before I had felt my options were limited.

Leaving paid employment meant my time became my own again and for the past eight years, I've been free to choose how I spend it without the constraints of having to work for someone else. I have numerous interests and especially enjoy travelling, speaking and writing because they stimulate my mind and offer opportunities for meaningful interactions with others.

A psychologist friend recently laughed at the irony of my becoming a financial success despite failing high school maths and economics and my becoming a writer when I had only scraped by in English. Wherever you have come from, no matter what your life experiences, you can expand your mind and improve your life. No matter what odds you think are stacked against you, what matters is the vision you hold of the person you wish to become. You choose both what you think and how you feel about what you think.

When you fully appreciate this freedom, and enjoy every step of progress you make along the way, you realise that it is not our destinations in life that matter as much as the adventures we experience on our way to reaching them.

The diversity of human thought and behaviour leads me to think of people as intrinsically interesting creatures with a seemingly limitless capacity to learn and grow, and it is this bottomless well of potential that inspires me to encourage others to flourish.

True freedom comes from our choice of thought because we have the capacity to select thoughts that lead us to feel positive emotion. The amount of freedom an individual experiences stems from their willingness to focus their thoughts and be guided by their feelings.

For years my self-limiting beliefs had me in a holding pattern. I kept thinking the same types of thoughts and getting the same types of results. Then I learned to shift my thinking into a state where great expectations have become natural to me.

It is my sincere wish that my ideas will add value to your life so that you can also choose to enjoy money and happiness in harmony.

Now allow me to take your imagination on a journey back in time.

Innocently imaginative
Stimulating the imagination you were born with

Imagination is everything. It is the preview of life's coming attractions.

Albert Einstein

Magic moments

The world can be a very magical place when you're six. I remember serving lemonade in a pink plastic tea set to a girl over the back fence. The tea set had come in my Santa sack, and I was keen to give it a trial run. Even though the teapot was only tiny and didn't hold much lemonade, I was delighted to be entertaining without the supervision of my mother.

Not long after this someone tried to enlighten me by telling me that Santa wasn't real. I thought they were deluded. I remained in denial, even when my older sister pointed out that it was more than a coincidence that Santa drank the same beer as my Dad. I figured that Santa was a nice guy and happy to drink what was on offer. The non-believers obviously didn't know what they were talking about. But once doubts about Santa began to surface, it wasn't long before the Easter bunny and the tooth fairy also came under scrutiny. You spend the first wonderful years of your life living in fairyland and then someone taps you on the shoulder and says, "That's only pretend. You're growing up now. Welcome to the real world".

Parents and teachers may have good intentions, but they can become a little tedious around this age. They tell you that you have to learn stuff and become more responsible. I was told I had to behave like a lady, do my homework and tidy my room. The list went on and on, and the enchantment in my life was in danger of slipping away.

But, as luck would have it, a very magical person entered my life and the impression she made stays with me to this day. She had a confident, no-nonsense air about her. She dressed in a slightly quirky way that said she was comfortable with who she was and didn't feel a need to conform. She had an amazing ability to bring people around to seeing her point of view. Her clever wit and enchanting personality captivated the attention of those around her. She always looked calm, cool and collected. She was imperturbable. I was hooked. When I grew up I wanted to be like her.

In my untarnished six-year-old imagination, my dream was to become a clever, capable, capricious and charming adult, just like my heroine. We even shared the same first name (in real life), which somehow made it seem more appropriate. I could see myself giving direction to those around me, just like Mary Poppins. I'd say things like, "We're going to do it my way, but it's okay, it's going to be fun!"

Dreams matter

Some things stand the test of time. Julie Andrews' performance as Mary Poppins sparked my imagination in a big way and the feelings it stirred within me are still with me today. Like great movies, some dreams survive while others fade.

Our dreams are stimulated from many sources. Your dreams, like some of mine, may come from your childhood or they may have appeared only yesterday. They may come from watching a movie or visiting the home of a friend. It doesn't matter where your dreams begin but it matters that you have them. Dreams are important because they are where success begins. All significant human achievement, including wealth creation, begins with desire that is kindled in our imagination.

For me, Mary Poppins was a great role model when I was six, but our dreams are often shaped from multiple sources and as time passed I needed to gather some more clues about the sort of person I wanted to become as an adult. Every now and then I would meet someone who would trigger something in my mind.

Stepping into a storybook

'Wow! This is huge', I thought to myself as I stood at the entrance to an enormous courtyard, at the centre of which was the largest private swimming pool I had ever seen. It had a diving board and a slippery dip and was immensely inviting to a keen swimmer like myself. The home was the type of residence I'd seen in movies but never before in real life. I was 12 years old at the time and seriously impressed.

The owner of this significant abode was Mr Arthur. He also owned a string of shops in the city, the largest of which was near Dad's pharmacy. He and Dad had become friends and, on this day, Mr Arthur had invited us to lunch. Following my brief assessment of his property, I decided that my Dad's friend must be loaded.

Mr Arthur made us feel very welcome. He was thoughtful and generous and not at all like the greedy rich people I had heard about. He had the means to enjoy life and took pleasure in sharing it with others. Dad told me that Mr Arthur had come to Australia as a teenager with no money and speaking very little English. Success had not been handed to him on a platter.

Before I left his house that day I gazed around at the magnificent surroundings. I decided that when I grew up I wanted to live in a big house with a beautiful swimming pool, just like Mr Arthur's. The day at his house was an enchanting experience for me, like stepping into a storybook.

Bringing desires and beliefs into harmony

Visiting Mr Arthur's house sparked my imagination and kindled within me a love of fine real estate and a desire to be wealthy, but I wasn't able to realise those dreams until I brought my desires, beliefs and expectations into harmony. For a time, as an adult, I lost sight of some of my dreams. I thought it was normal to worry about not having enough money. I wasn't fully aware of the negative beliefs I had adopted on the subject of money until I began to pay more attention to people who were more comfortable with it.

When the thought of, or the discussion of, money conjures up negative emotion, it indicates that there is a conflict between what a person wants and what they believe they can have. I had some self-limiting beliefs but managed to manoeuvre my mind towards a much more self-empowering viewpoint and the first step was using my imagination to explore new possibilities.

It is often not until we grow tired of feeling pushed around by circumstances that we make a decision to change the direction of our life and pursue our dreams. When I decided to accumulate investment properties, some people warned me not to dream too big. I'm so glad I didn't listen to them. I now know that it is not the size of your dreams that is important. What is important is that you pursue dreams that excite you. Imagination and passion are key factors in bringing desires and beliefs into harmony.

Dream stealers

The adult image I created when I was a child was challenged on many fronts as I grew. We come into this life with a clean slate but, little by little, the world and the people around us put limitations on us. Though these may be by well-meaning loved ones, the limitations they impose are often based on their own life experiences and not always relevant to us. If you're lucky, you get to play with your imagination for a few years before it gets squashed down to a size that the adults around you feel comfortable with.

But though it may feel tempting to blame others for stomping on our dreams, this type of thinking is contrary to our inherent desire to feel free. **How can you achieve your dreams when you feel that someone or something is inhibiting your freedom?** No one can steal your dreams when you choose not to give credit to the negative opinions of others. The opinion that matters most is your own.

You control what you imagine

Sometimes we can be our own worst enemy. I've had times when I've worried, *What if I'm not quite good enough? What if I make a mistake?* Or, heaven forbid, *What if I fail?* But this type of thinking never *felt* good. What does feel good is when I establish the emotion I want to feel and adjust my self-talk accordingly and there are stories in the chapters that follow that will lead you to a greater understanding of how I achieve this. My dreams have a habit of coming true when I consistently practice paying attention to the way I feel and *choosing* thoughts that *feel* better.

I use the words adjusting and shifting because our brains are not static. We are born with active responsive minds and I've learned that procrastinating or avoiding change only leads to stagnation, frustration or worse. The more we acknowledge and utilise our ability to shift our focus and alter our viewpoint, the easier it is to make decisions. Even seemingly small or insignificant decisions can be of value if they take you closer to believing you can achieve your dreams.

When we ignore our fear or pretend it doesn't matter, it inhibits our natural expansion. If we stay in denial for too long, the pressure that builds up will affect our wellbeing in some way or another. When we get stuck in strong beliefs and rigid views our imagination shrinks and this can lead us to think we don't have much control. That's when it is most convenient to blame others or circumstances for our misfortune. But I discovered true freedom when I realised the only person capable of stealing my dreams was me. Dreams have a habit of remaining out of reach until we acknowledge that we control what we think about *and* **what we imagine**.

Open-minded innocence

Why is it that young children learn so much faster than adults? Could it be their open-minded innocence and that they are unbiased about what is possible, relaxed and playful enough to be creative, and patient enough to pace themselves and persevere through learning curves? Or is it that as adults we become bound up in self-limiting beliefs that stifle our naturally creative nature?

We are all born with an imagination and it thrives naturally when we are children. When a baby takes its first steps and falls over, it doesn't give up. It gets up and has another go. Although their first attempts may be imperfect they persevere, one step at a time, until they reach a point of unconscious competence where they no longer need to think about the process. They practice walking until running becomes the next logical step.

Three lessons about money

I was not taught how to *make* money at school. I was taught how to put myself in a position to *earn* money. I had friends who put enormous time and effort into their formal education yet I noticed that some earned less than others. Friends with similar qualifications did not always have similar incomes.

When I began to mix with people who were financially savvy, I noticed that some of them had little or no formal education. Some were high school drop-outs. They were not typically any one personality type and had varying upbringings. This challenged some of my self-limiting beliefs.

There had been times when I'd been afraid of trying things because I didn't want to admit what I didn't know. I wanted to avoid making mistakes and appearing foolish, but this attitude limited my opportunities to learn and grow. I realised I needed to keep an open mind.

Although I did not undertake a formal course that came with a study plan, I did eventually give considerable focus to my financial education. I did not have a methodical approach but managed to pace myself as I persevered through learning curves, mastering smaller steps before I gathered momentum.

As my confidence grew, I became more easy going and was more easily able to release my self-limiting beliefs. Many were fixed ideas that I had clung to for years that had kept me small and inhibited my free spirit; many were ideas that I'd adopted from society and considered to be *common knowledge*.

Like common sense, I was realising that knowledge is only useful if it serves you.

So my first lesson about money was that the attainment of wealth is not common to a particular personality type, socioeconomic background or educational qualification. It is available to everyone. When it comes to creating wealth, the only limitations are in the mind of the perceiver.

My second lesson was that if I wanted to achieve something extraordinary, I had to open my mind. I surrounded myself with inspirational material and limited my exposure to negative messages about money. I gradually became less concerned with what was probable and more entertained by **what** was possible.

My third lesson was that wealth can be created. This was good news because I realised I didn't have to compete for money that was perceived to already be in existence. Money is only scarce when you imagine it is. I think of it like this. I don't run to an open window every morning sucking in fresh air in case it runs out later in the day.

Three steps to a wealthy mind
- *Release self-limiting beliefs*
- *Open your mind*
- *Use your imagination to shift from a perception of limitation to one of abundance*

Envisioning your success

We can use our imagination to blow things up out of all proportion or shrink things down into insignificance. We can create wonderful visions and scenarios in our mind's eye or worry about terrible things that may never actually happen.

When we experience tough times, it is easy to get confused and think that we don't have much control over what happens to us and, for a while, I thought some people were just lucky. When I made excuses or avoided taking responsibility for my choices, my options shrank and so did the creative potential of my mind.

For a time I thought *you can't have it all*, but now I have a different view. You can have it all. You can have anything you want and it all starts in your imagination. Our imagination is a powerful tool as it is the place where we design our destiny. We get to choose what is playing on the screen of our mind. When we are worrying, life tends to present us with something to worry about. When we are appreciating, life tends to present us with more things to appreciate. When we are excited about our dreams, life tends to present us with more things to become excited about.

Some people may encourage you to set realistic goals and not to dream too big, for fear of being disappointed or disillusioned. My view is that the only limitation you should place on your dreams is that they be of your own design and imagining. No one else can measure your dreams and know whether they are right or wrong or too big or small. Only you can know what feels right for you.

Finding the right emotional charge

Imagination may seem most related to our sense of sight, yet it also involves how we feel. In our mind's eye we can envision people we want to meet, places we want to be or things we want to have, but the key to bringing our desires to fruition is the emotional stance that those images conjure.

If you desire to become wealthy you may see yourself as having more money, but unless you can make a positive emotional connection as you paint those pictures, they will remain just dreams. Dreams become reality when the dream *feels* right. You may be painting the right pictures but feeling fearful. If you are afraid of losing money, you'll have a hard time trying to make it. Finding the right emotional charge is often the missing piece of the puzzle.

The jigsaw of success

Achieving financial freedom was like putting together a jigsaw puzzle. Even when I thought I couldn't have it all, I was still unknowingly gathering the clues to my success. Little pieces of my life experience were filed away ready to be utilised at an opportune time. When I began to really use the power of my imagination, I had lots of things stored in my mind's filing cabinet. Ideas were just sitting there waiting for me to tune in.

Imagine these pages are like a magnet. Let them draw out great things from within you. Allow them to delve deep into the filing cabinet of your mind and arouse your thoughts and stimulate your mind's eye.

Allow memories to bubble to the surface as you remember little bits of yourself that you may have forgotten. Even if you feel that you haven't exercised your imagination very much lately, that's okay. I'm sure it's still there. It might just need a little stimulation.

Dreams that motivate

The reason I am presenting glimpses of my childhood dreams is to remind you of the potential of our imaginings. I remember visiting my grandmother's house when I was a kid. It opened doors in my mind. She and my aunt told stories of their trips to faraway places. The world was a much more mysterious place back then, without computers or the internet. Information was not as instantly available as it is today. I remember looking at their photos and listening intently to the descriptions they gave. I imagined myself packing a bag and going on adventures to exotic locations.

In my adult life I have managed to achieve these dreams and many more. I live in an idyllic location, mix with amazing people, travel to exotic locations every year, and work, when I crave mental stimulation, on projects that hold great interest for me. I now cherish the dreams that gave me the initial motivation to grow financially. It is much easier to focus on making money when you have a specific purpose for it.

Our desires and dreams are the basis of our motivation for wanting more of anything. You wouldn't be reading this if you didn't want more of something. My dreams gave me motivation as an adult to become financially savvy. If you want more money, open your mind to new possibilities. To achieve your dreams you've got to be prepared to expand your thinking and exercise your imagination.

The potential of our imagination is so immense there is a big chance that you are underestimating yours right now. Imagine designing your life exactly as you would like it. Can you picture yourself having the types of relationships you wish to foster? Can you see yourself enjoying greater happiness and prosperity?

Dare to dream up your perfect world with no limits. Let your imagination run free. You do not need to take any action right now except to allow yourself to become innocently imaginative. This book is designed to help you to build your vision up to a point where you feel compelled to act, not through fear, but with unbridled enthusiasm; a point of ***knowing*** when the action feels so right that you couldn't imagine yourself doing anything else.

Exercise your imagination
- *Take some time out to relax and daydream a little. Just take long enough to think about some areas of your life that you want to improve. Don't spend too long on this. This is not a planning exercise. There is no need to think about how you are going to achieve these things but simply identify* **what** *you want.*
- *Focus on the* **what** *and the* **why**, *not on the 'how'. The reason for this is that the 'how' comes naturally when you are very clear about the* **what** *and the* **why**. *Many people don't achieve big goals because they get hung up on the 'how' way too early.*
- *Write down* **what** *you want and the reasons* **why** *you want it. Then sit quietly, close your eyes and spend a couple of minutes imagining how your life will be better once you have achieved your dreams.*

Our imaginings pre-pave our future

If you are a sanguine type, this exercise will probably make enormous sense because of your naturally optimistic leaning and the ease with which you use your imagination. If however, the initial value of this does not strike a chord, *relax*. There are numerous prompts and exercises throughout the book that are designed to stimulate your imagination.

Your desires shape *who you are becoming* and are crucial to your expansion. Defining what you desire brings clarity of focus of thought. Knowing why you want something kindles your emotions. The more enthusiastic you are about your subject of focus, the more likely you are to achieve your dreams and desires.

You were born with a powerful imagination and, even if you think you are not a creative type, you have the ability to become one. The value in being creative is that you can set the scene for future scenarios in your head. Rather than taking what life dishes out, you can take greater control of where your life is heading.

Take yourself back in time

Picture yourself as a child again. Remember a time when you were playing and got lost in the world of your own imagination. Rediscover that innocent part of yourself which is capable of dreaming with pure desire, untainted by anyone else's views or expectations. Who do you see yourself becoming? How will your life be better?

During my childhood I didn't know that my imagination would play such a big part in my future success. Mary Poppins had left the building by the time I was 12. But becoming an adult was a little way off yet. I was about to become a teenager and my brain, as I had known it, was also about to leave the building.

Invincibility of the mind
Developing resilient thinking

What would you do if you weren't afraid?
           from *Who Moved My Cheese?* by Dr Spencer Johnson.

Adopting invincible thinking

Some may consider that invincibility is about how you act or behave but, for me, invincibility is about how you think. It is not about dominance over others but rather about having control over your own thoughts. People are often so concerned with **what** they should do. *Am I making the right choice? What if I make a mistake?*

Because our actions are a result of our thoughts, it makes sense to work on adopting invincible thinking **before** you try to make any significant changes in your life. It is much easier to first change your thinking than to try and change what you are doing. When you improve the quality of your thinking, your actions will naturally follow suit and give you better results.

Budding investors often ask me questions about the **action** I took to acquire a property portfolio that sustains my lifestyle. Their questions, and their demeanour, generally indicate their level of knowledge and confidence. While knowledge is valuable, I have met many a would-be investor who has researched extensively and yet still has little confidence. They are waiting for the perfect conditions or the ideal investment because they are afraid of getting it wrong.

As I launched into property investing, I worked on expanding my thinking, so when it came to making big decisions I wasn't looking for someone to hold my hand or tell me what to do. There were times when I was uncertain, but a little uncertainty is normal on any learning curve. It adds to the excitement factor. When life is predictable it can become boring.

Once my big picture was planted firmly in my mind, options became more obvious. When I became clear about my greater goals, it was easier to trust my instincts and allow my enthusiasm to carry me toward more answers.

When you develop the ability to manoeuvre your mind, decision making becomes easier because you are less worried about making mistakes. As you increase your ability to weave your way through the ever-changing landscape of life towards your desired outcomes, the choices you make and the actions you take seem not only natural but are often compelling.

Early inklings of invincibility came when I was a teenager, at a time when I became increasingly interested in making my own decisions and less inclined to blindly follow the advice of others. There have been many times since then that I have forgotten this irresistible state of mind, times when I felt that my decisions should be based on what I thought would be acceptable or pleasing to others. This is not to say that I don't care about what others think, but more that I had to remember how important it is to first pay attention to how *I* feel about what I am thinking and what I am doing.

Invincibility suggests an absence of fear and, as I pondered how to best describe ways to obtain this type of thinking and maintain it on a regular basis, the following stories came to mind. They serve as a reminder of how to apply simple concepts to our complex lives.

Learning from our youth

The teenage mind is a source of fascination for me and I have learned valuable lessons having had the benefit of looking at it from two vantage points: one as an adult observing and the other as an adult remembering. Living with six teenagers coming and going in and out of my household for the past dozen years has challenged me to understand a teenager's way of thinking.

At times I fell into the trap of thinking that because I was *the adult* that I knew better or that I knew what was good for them. I tried to introduce rules like: *Be home by midnight. Do your homework. Keep your room tidy.* But there was a strange irony in making rules for someone else when I hate being told what to do.

As a teenager, when I went out I didn't want to have to be home by midnight, I'd always hated homework and there were times when keeping my bedroom neat was not a priority. It caused me to question why any human being would want to make **rules** for another. It is so much easier to influence rather than to try to control.

Rules can restrict our sense of freedom so I now prefer to think of them as guidelines or suggestions. This approach makes enormous sense when you consider that each individual on the planet makes their own set of rules and, like people, no two sets are exactly alike—**rules are individual.**

Another lesson I learned from our teenagers had to do with worrying less and trusting more. Worrying about my children (or anyone) has never ever helped them or me. I couldn't be *worried* **and** *helpful* at the same time. And despite my worrying, the resilience of our teenagers continued to astound me. They generally didn't take life nearly as seriously as I sometimes did and spent less time worrying about the future and more time living in the moment.

I tried to remember myself as a teenager so I could understand their attitude but didn't always take into account the fact that I was now an adult with a lot more life experience, a broader view of life and the benefit of hindsight. On top of that, our teenagers were living in a different, newer world, full of an ever-growing variety of choices. I couldn't expect them to see things my way but their carefree approach inspired me to try to see things their way and, rather serendipitously, the universe eventually provided me with an unexpected glimpse back in time.

While moving house I found a stack of my old diaries. I laughed out loud as I read some pages from my latter teenage years. I was impulsive and busy living in the moment. If something wasn't fun, I wasn't interested. There was no **to do** list, just **today** moments.

These insights helped me to understand why teenagers often appear invincible or fearless compared to older generations. We all have the potential to experience a more exuberant life that brings feelings of invincibility but, like many simple things, we forget. As we mature, our minds can become more cluttered and we can become distracted trying to cover so many bases.

Can you recall times when you have felt invincible; moments when you've been so excited about what you were doing you couldn't imagine doing anything else? Teenagers tend to achieve this state more often because their minds are less crowded and their outlook on life more straightforward. When you live in the moment you allow more scope for spontaneity and adventure.

School daze

Becoming a teenager can be like a double-edged sword. You get a taste of freedom when you're away from adult supervision, but you're regularly reminded that the world is full of rules and restrictions and that can make you feel constrained.

There are aspects of my teenage thinking that I now admire. I cherish the part of myself that was craving to be an individual, was brave enough to dare to be different and adventurous enough to try new things and stretch myself a little. I sometimes chose to ignore rules that I felt weren't relevant to me. I thought the rules were there to give people who were afraid a justification for their fear. The rules only applied if you chose to acknowledge the fear-based thinking that created them.

During this time, significant character traits were emerging in me. Though my parents encouraged me to study, I was much more interested in my peers than my school work. Despite my lack of academic enthusiasm, school provided an ideal environment for social interaction and, as I observed my teenage peers and the adults around me, I became fascinated with what made them tick.

Why were some luckier, funnier, or more clever than others? Why were some girls at school bitchy while others were friendly? Why did some people want to bring you down when you were flying high, while others applauded and encouraged the moments when you shone? It didn't occur to me at the time that self-awareness and a strong interest in and understanding of others would contribute so significantly to my future success.

A taste of the limelight

Having a bunch of nuns determine my dress code for a significant portion of my school life seemed a strange irony. It wasn't that I was a fashion guru, it was more that I couldn't understand why we had to take direction about the way we presented ourselves from a group of women who wore the same shapeless black-and-white outfits day in, day out.

The college I attended had oodles of rules and uniform regulations were strict. We had to wear blazers, hats and gloves when we were outside the school grounds. We weren't allowed to wear jewellery or make-up and the nuns would police the bus stops each afternoon to make sure we were looking and behaving like ladies.

Wanting to break the bonds of the goody-two-shoes Catholic girl look, I experimented with hair colour. I dyed my hair bright red one week and purple the next. Although some of my friends seemed suitably impressed by my attempts at self-expression, I was not the first girl to do this. Bright red or purple hair was not the norm but it had been done before.

Wanting to take it one step further, I decided to trial a new look. I went to the supermarket and purchased several bottles of green food dye and went home to apply it to my long locks. Green hair colouring products were scarce in the early '70s, so I had to use my ingenuity.

Although I was normally a quiet non-achiever, I did have a few attention-grabbing moments, and this one was memorable. Green food colour doesn't do much for hair manageability, so I arrived at school with no time to spare, looking like I had a bright-green feather duster on my head.

Intending to make a quick dash to my classroom just in time for roll-call, I came barrelling around the corner into the big quadrangle to the sudden realisation that this morning there was a special full school assembly. I tried to blend into the back of the crowd, my hat in my hand. Then I saw her glaring at me. It was Sister Mary Scary and she looked really mean. I wondered why she was looking meaner than usual. In my rush I'd forgotten what I must have looked like. I may as well have had a flashing beacon on my head.

*From the look on her face I figured I would wind up in detention for a week. But then she smiled her scariest smile and walked towards me. She told me to follow her and she marched straight up to the platform at the front of the assembly to parade me in front of the whole school as an example of what **not** to look like. This was attention grabbing on a much larger scale than I had planned.*

Caring about how you feel

Although I felt a little awestruck as I saw the sea of faces looking up at me from the assembly, by the end of that day I was so glad that I'd made an effort to express myself. The monotony of sameness drove me crazy. I got a bit more limelight than I'd bargained on, but it was blissful having a day out of the ordinary. Observing reactions from classmates and teachers was enjoyable. Some scowled, probably thinking I had green colouring on the brain, yet for each frown there were many more smiles and admiring glances.

Episodes like this are significant because I did something that was fun and felt right for me, even though it was outside the comfort zone of others. **Invincibility comes from worrying less about what others are thinking and caring more about what you are feeling.** It felt good to play by my own rules. I figured as long as I wasn't hurting anyone else, I should be able to do as I please.

Not long after my green hair-scapade, I wagged school for a day with a friend. Someone reported us and my parents were called to the school. Sister Mary Scary was really angry. She went so red in the face I thought she was going to explode.

My desire to feel free often overrode pressure from society to conform. Wagging school was exciting. It felt like the right thing to do at the time and, even though it nearly got me expelled, I look back with no regrets.

Making my own rules

Feelings of invincibility can be very powerful when you are a teenager and for me it was a time to test boundaries and question rules. I was intrigued as to why one person can engage in dangerous antics and thrive, yet another seemingly careful individual can meet with disaster doing something ordinary or mundane. I wondered why we are encouraged to make safe choices based on statistics or the experiences or opinions of others, when my observation of successful people is that they take risks and make choices based on their own comfort zone rather than that of the crowd. The thrill is not so much in breaking the rules but in learning to make your own.

The big washing machine

"Get your mat. We're going," directed the voice on the other end of the phone. *"But the weather is awful,"* I protested. It was a wildly windy day with drizzle angling its way through the gusts. Not exactly beach weather, but my friend was too excited to care. *"The waves are 12 to 15-feet high, Julie. We can't miss this!"*

At the age of 14, one of my favourite activities was spending time on weekends at the beach with my friends, riding waves on my surf mat. It gave me a sense of freedom and was something I enjoyed that wasn't breaking any rules. But this day was different. The beach was officially closed. I considered this fact only briefly. The prospect of riding a 12 to 15-foot swell had stirred my sense of adventure. Together with two girlfriends, I headed for the surf.

We arrived at the beach and stood for a while admiring the powerful oversized waves. From experience, we knew it would be hard to get past these giants with our surf mats inflated so we folded them under one arm and plunged into the chilly water.

Making it past the breakers proved to be exhausting. Once we'd caught our breath, we inflated our mats, keeping a watchful eye on the approaching waves. The sets were erratic but once we were out that far it was too late to change our minds.

We decided the quickest way back to shore was to ride our mats so when a massive wave approached we all paddled like crazy to catch it in the right spot. Feeling the exhilaration of shooting down the wave I thought I was home free, but then it broke right on top of me. I instinctively abandoned my mat and dived down deep to get underneath the force of the surge. But this wave was more powerful than any I had experienced before. I considered myself a strong swimmer, but I felt like a piece of fluff caught in a giant washing machine. The surf had swallowed me up and wouldn't let me go.

I struggled to break free but the turbulence of the water had me in a spin, swirling out of control. I felt panic rising up within me, knowing I needed to get some air fast. My lungs felt like they were going to burst. I suddenly felt exhausted and the effort was almost too much. It was so tempting to rest and let go. A part of me wanted desperately to release myself from struggle, but I knew I had to breathe soon or I would drown.

I faced a choice of life or death. I could give up the fight or find the strength to swim for my life. It was then that I noticed daylight above me. Having become completely disoriented, recognising the direction of the surface was a saving grace. My focus shifted. I made my choice.

Swimming with a steely determination towards the light, I broke the surface for long enough to gulp a little air and a lot of water, and was sucked back under several more times. Finally, I broke the surface for long enough to see the beach. I swam with all my might towards the shore until I was able to dig my feet into the sand and hold my position.

A figure waded into the water towards me. He grabbed my arm and pulled me onto the beach. I was gasping for breath and my long hair was hanging like a mop in front of my face. When I pushed it back I realised my bikini was not in the same place it had been when I had entered the water. Thankfully the guy politely pretended not to notice as I pulled *myself together. Within minutes a hysterical voice pierced the air. One of my friends was scurrying towards me looking bedraggled. Before long we found our mate further up the beach. Both girls, like me, looked like drowned rats and had a wild look in their eyes.*

The freedom to focus our thoughts

Although this incident nearly made me a candidate for the Darwin Awards[1], I have no regrets. Some may think that this is an example of why we should obey rules but the experience made me realise how much I wanted to live. Although I was young and physically fit at the time, I believe that it was my strength of mind that day that saved my life.

There are times in life, like this, when you feel that your choices of action are limited and it is easy to forget that **your choice of thought is vast**. We are free to choose what we think about and free to choose our focus. When I was swirling out of control, caught in the force of the wave, I felt overwhelmed. I was physically out of control and it scared me. The enormous physical exertion exhausted me to the point where I wanted to stop and rest, and the memory of that moment is still crystal clear in my mind. But I felt that I had a choice of whether to live or die. I had a choice of focusing on living or thinking about dying.

Once I made that choice I ***knew*** that I would make it back onto the beach and live to swim another day. When you manage to conjure a strong, clear, emotionally-charged picture in your mind of what you want, your physical body can't help but follow suit. Some could cast this story aside saying that I was just lucky. But those who understand the power of focus of the human mind will know that we create our own luck. This powerful focus is exactly the same type of thinking that enabled me to achieve financial freedom. I made a decision and ***knew*** that I would achieve my

---

1 The Awards honour people who ensure the long-term survival of the human race by removing themselves from the gene pool in a sublimely idiotic fashion.

goal because of the vision I held in my mind. At times like this my ***knowing*** is more like an intense feeling than a thought.

In his book *Think and Grow Rich,* Napoleon Hill speaks of having a "definite major purpose". When I speak with other investors, I occasionally meet one who is extremely clear about where they are heading. I can see it in their eyes and hear the conviction in their voice. They display a confidence or ***knowing*** that speaks of success. They have a definite major purpose and a clear focus. They have nailed exactly what they want and their enthusiasm is intoxicating.

> *Excitement and enthusiasm drive us forward into the arms of opportunity. Fear holds us back and can keep us in shackles, in a place where we are afraid of the depth of our imagination. Fear stifles the passion that is our birthright and diminishes the energy that causes us to thrive naturally and freely. When we shift from fear into excitement, we engage in the natural flow of energy that is life itself.*

From fear to focus and freedom

My fondest memories of myself as a teenager are times when I felt irresistibly invincible but as I grew into an adult I became aware of so many things people become fearful about. We can become fearful of death, loneliness, illness, injury, scarcity or failure. The list is endless. Our media abounds with stories of ways to contract illness, lose money or die in some spectacular fashion. Every day people are murdered, robbed, ridiculed, infected, used and abused. It's enough to scare anyone who chooses to give it too much attention.

Fear is an emotional response to what we are thinking and our thoughts are often a response to what we are observing. Fear is useful in helping us to identify what we don't want but that is where its usefulness ends. When we dwell in a fearful state for too long, it inhibits our growth. You cannot improve a situation by worrying about it. So how do you turn off the fear tap and turn your mind in the direction of what you want? Once you have identified what you don't want, focus **only** on what you **do** want.

There is great freedom in learning to quickly manoeuvre your thoughts away from fearful ones towards what you desire and there are tactics throughout this book that will strengthen your ability to do this. A clear focus or decision can save you from fear. In my adult life I have had so many choices and so much time to make them, I sometimes got lost in a land of procrastination. When I was in the surf that day I had no time to procrastinate. The urgency of the situation demanded a snappy decision.

Procrastination stems from a fear of making the wrong choice. As an adult I learned the art of procrastinating down to a tee and wasted lots of time avoiding making decisions and therefore taking my chances with what life dished out. When I learned to shift my thinking from fearful thoughts, worrying about making wrong choices or mistakes (things I don't want) and focused more clearly and definitely on my desires (what I do want) my life has taken one positive turn after another.

Now I can look back with no regrets knowing that life is all about making choices. Every decision we make takes us to a new vantage point.

The good thing about fear is that it provides an indicator of what we don't want and it is often not until you really nail what you don't want that you become crystal clear about what it is that you do want. And if you think this means becoming driven, think again. I have a lazy streak. Why do you think I wanted to give up working for a wage? I enjoy working on projects that I am enthusiastic about but I don't relate to those who say you must be driven to achieve your goals. When my mind is on the right wavelength, my body naturally flows in the direction of my goals.

Our minds are flexible enough to make many choices possible. We can choose to be afraid of dying or choose to be excited by living. Worrying about a lack of money doesn't make people rich, just as worrying about sickness doesn't make people healthy. We don't get what we want while our attention is focused on what we don't want.

When you make a decision about what you **do want** you feel empowered. **When you find the right focus it feeds feelings of freedom,** and you can rediscover your natural exuberance and give yourself permission to thrive!

> *Risk and opportunity usually travel together. Where some perceive risk, others see opportunity. The thrill of life happens out on the skinny branches because that is where the fruit is!*

Manoeuvrability of the mind is about utilising our emotions as an indicator or an opportunity to shift our thinking. The idea is to quickly recognise when you are feeling negative emotion, on any subject, and to direct your thoughts to things that will help you to improve your emotional standpoint. A positive emotional standpoint is where we do our best work, when we thrive and shine. That's why it's important to look for reasons to feel good, as often as you think of it, each day. It is an incredibly simple yet unbelievably empowering way to live your life: so simple yet so easy to forget or undervalue.

The amount of freedom an individual enjoys has much to do with their ability to manoeuvre their mind. We are free to find value or find fault, free to appreciate or condemn, free to admire or to criticise.

Success and happiness happen in our thoughts and in our imagination **before** they can appear in our life. And our emotions are there to guide us. When you are scared of something, it is better to change the way you are thinking **before** you take action. When you learn to manoeuvre your thoughts in response to what you are feeling, you can put your mind into a place where you have nothing to fear.

Humans can be impatient creatures. Sometimes we want it all **now**. Waiting for our dreams to come to fruition can seem frustrating. When we remember to be happy with small improvements and enjoy every little bit of progress along the way, the momentum builds. Start with small steps and take bigger steps as your thinking progresses, and look for that winning edge no matter how small a window it might seem.

Invincibility is a state of mind. When you build an invincible mindset you understand that failure is only temporary. Opportunity lies around the corner of every mistake, every failure and every challenge. We are not born into this world to live in fear. We are born into this world to move beyond our fears, so that we can live out our dreams. Fearful thoughts can hold us back from living our life to the full and becoming the person we really want to be.

Are you drowning in fear or swimming towards your next breath? If you want to experience greater freedom in your life, more choice and more fun, learn to manoeuvre your mind away from fear towards the freedom that focus can bring. The concept of manoeuvrability of the mind is a complex one, and for this reason, the thread of it continues throughout the book.

What does freedom mean to you?

For me, freedom means having time and money to enjoy life, having fun, working when I feel like it, playing when I want to, enjoying wonderful relationships with family, friends and colleagues and continuing to find new things, people and places to get excited about.

The freedom to change our thinking and/or shift our focus gives us the power to improve the way we feel about any subject. It is this freedom that gives us control over our own life experience. We can choose to focus on things we don't want and feel bad, or focus on things we want and feel eager and excited. No one else can control what you think or how you feel about what you think. You can allow yourself to be influenced by others but, ultimately, you choose your own thoughts.

When you hold a belief that someone outside of yourself has power over you and can affect your life experience, you are giving up your freedom. Real freedom lies in first acknowledging and embracing your ability to choose your thoughts and thereby control the way you feel about life.

The more you exercise this freedom the more you feel alive, enthused and excited by life.

Fortune favours those who are bold enough to grab life experience, one episode after another, so they can continually identify new preferences and use their mind, with their emotions and instincts as guides, to manoeuvre their way towards more of what they want.

> **Build feelings of invincibility**
> - *Make a list of things you would like to change about your life.*
> - *What would it take to make you feel free?*
> - *What would you do if you had nothing to fear?*
>
> Even when you perceive that your choices of action are limited, **your choice of thought is vast**.

Ignorance can be blissful

When we feel invincible, we launch into life with fervour and enthusiasm. To feel invincible we need an open mind untarnished by fear. Children and teenagers often achieve this naturally through their blissful ignorance.

As children we get lost in the world of our imagination; as teenagers we are trying to make sense of the adult world. As our personality and character traits are taking shape, parents and teachers try to get us to conform and to obey rules, but sometimes the rules don't make sense because they are based on others' experiences and not our own.

In my teenage years I was much less concerned about consequences. It was sometimes my ignorance that allowed me to feel invincible. My sense of fun was much greater than my sense of fear. Looking back, I realise how much fear crept into my mind as I matured: *What if this happens? What if that happens? What if I'm not clever enough?* It took a number of years, but as I got over the what-ifs, I began to recognise that fear was one of the barriers that stood in the way of my success.

On leaving school I became afraid that I might be thought a failure. My choice was to either live in fear of being stupid or to work out how I could become smarter. Failing at school left me feeling a little less invincible, but I was about to discover another essential element of success.

Incurably optimistic
Adopting a buoyant attitude

Your attitude, not your aptitude, will determine your altitude.

Zig Ziglar

A somewhat pessimistic colleague once challenged the value of self-help books, saying that there was nothing new and that it was the same concepts being regurgitated. Having read many self-help and inspirational books, I have a different view. Although a concept like optimism may be familiar to the reader, the material is presented in different ways and also received on different levels. We obtain a greater benefit when we are open to receiving the messages.

Prompted by my success in real estate, budding investors often seem fixated on finding out what action I took so they can copy what I did, expecting to get the same results. But as they do this they overlook the most important factors: my attitude and emotional standpoint that caused me to take the action in the first place. That is why the snippets of my life experience prior to this time, that are related herein, are of such value.

Innate optimism

We are born with a natural optimism that can be stifled as we mature. When I was a kid my mother often joked that I always landed on my feet and my aunt used to reckon I wandered around looking at the world through rose-coloured glasses. When they first said this I didn't really know what they meant. I came to understand that my tendency to view the world around me in the best possible light was not something everyone else shared to the same extent. But as I grew, life threw more challenges my way and my optimism was put to the test more and more.

Other people's opinions and experiences do not always feed our optimism. Believing that limited academic achievement would restrict not only my career options, but also my earning capacity, I spent years working for ordinary wages. But in those years there were things I was learning that were pre-paving the way to my success. Sometimes we learn things before we find a reason to use the knowledge.

A small advantage can make a big difference

Enduring boring classes was something I'd hoped to leave behind in school. But in line with the commonly held belief that some additional formal education might redeem my past failures, I enrolled in a year-long secretarial course. Some of the classes were tedious, some were mediocre and others, like grooming and deportment, were downright stuffy.

But there was one class that really sparked my interest and that was psychology. I liked the teacher and he presented simple yet stimulating material that prompted my early interest in the subject. Observing people and developing an understanding of what motivates them to behave in certain ways was far more fascinating to me than anything else the course had to offer.

On the day of my final typing examination, I again had cause to question my suitability for formal education. I misread the timetable and showed up half an hour late. My typing speed was good but not good enough to make up for a lost 30 minutes. Failing typing meant no certificate.

My blasé attitude had again caused me to miss what others may have considered to be a good opportunity. But in my mind the year was far from a waste of time. I had enjoyed my introduction to the subject of psychology immensely, and that small advantage alone made a big impression on me.

And the secretarial course was not my only learning curve that year. While working part-time in my Dad's pharmacy in the city I learned some valuable people skills. One of the girls who trained me was extremely upbeat in her outlook on life. She demonstrated the immense advantages that come from serving people with a friendly smile and a helpful attitude.

A refined focus

Despite failing secretarial college, I set off in blissful ignorance and scored my first full-time job. For all the things I failed to learn at school, I did understand the importance of creating a favourable impression at a job interview.

Earning full-time pay, I soon discovered how much fun it was to have and spend money in larger quantities. New options were presenting themselves and for a while I spent with carefree abandon. But I soon I realised that when our intentions are weak we are vulnerable to the will of others.

When I had no clear direction or focus, I found there were plenty of people, in all types of business, who were ready to relieve me of my money.

When I made the decision that I would save to go overseas it felt great to have a definite purpose for my money rather than squandering it on things that would soon be forgotten. It is much easier to be optimistic about money when you are excited about spending it on something that is meaningful to you.

As I was unsure where to begin, my Dad encouraged me to make some enquiries. I priced a return flight to London, a three-week tour of Europe and different types of Eurail pass. I also researched travel books so I could estimate how much I would need for food and accommodation on a daily basis. I was then able to calculate approximately how much spending money I would need for several months away.

This was my first significant financial plan, figuring out how much money I needed for the trip and estimating how long it would take me to save up, based on my income and expenses. It was a simple yet powerful exercise.

Having fun with my friends was still a priority but I knew from my year at college that I didn't need to spend a lot of money to have a good time. With my travel goal firmly planted in my mind, I stuck to my savings plan, resisting temptation to spend the money on other things. I daydreamed of how excited I'd feel when the day came to get on the plane.

Plenty of my school friends had echoed my desire to travel, but after all the talk at school, only one saved up enough to make the journey. It took us both over a year but when it came time to buy our tickets we were thrilled.

The big bar up in the sky

"More champagne?" asked the stewardess as she leaned over my nearly empty glass. I smiled and tilted my glass toward the bottle. I was sitting in the first class lounge of a 747 wondering if this was how people travelled in heaven. We ate so much food we thought we were going to burst. I had flown before but never in such style.

A friend of my Dad had arranged that my friend Linda and I could spend the first leg of the journey being given the royal treatment. We were escorted up a spiral staircase and got to meet the pilot and crew. This was even better than I had imagined. After an action-packed month travelling around Europe together, Linda decided to stay in London with family and I headed for adventure.

A taste of freedom

Venturing off on my own was the most exciting feeling. It was 1978, long before email, internet cafes and mobile phones. With no firm plans I knew I was going to be untraceable for a while and although I missed my family I felt an immense sense of freedom. I had no one to answer to. I could do whatever I wanted and travel to any location I felt like. Although I was travelling on a budget I had enough money to see me through for a couple more months away. The mystery of not knowing where I was heading was enticing and the feeling of freedom I experienced is still fresh in my mind.

By the age of 23 I had taken several extended overseas trips. My dreams of travelling were being realised and this was a direct result of my optimism and refined focus.

Optimism carries us toward our dreams and our sense of freedom strengthens as we acknowledge every little triumph along the way

The value of daydreams

As a child were you ever told not to daydream? I remember gazing out of the window of my classroom in primary school, dreaming of being somewhere else; somewhere more exciting and interesting than my classroom was to me at that time.

As we grow into adults we are often discouraged from daydreaming because it is viewed as a waste of time. There have been times when I was led to believe it was for simple or lazy minds. Now I have come to understand its value. We function at our best potential when we are feeling good about ourselves, feeling good about what we're doing and where we're heading.

Remember the exercise at the end of Chapter 2 where I encouraged you to take some time out to relax and daydream a little. This is the sort of thing that will help you to recapture the little child within, so you can gaze off into the windows of your future and see the sort of things you want to see; imagine places you would like to be; picture the sort of people you would like to meet; dream of the person you are becoming. It will still be you, but an expanded and broader version of who you are now.

In daydreams we can dream up the best mix of what we want our future to hold. We can use our imagination to design our life the way we want it. This is touched upon in greater detail in upcoming chapters when we look deeper into the magnetic power of the mind.

Daydreaming is an opportunity to renovate your life and paint the best possible scenarios. If you were going to renovate your home, would you first picture the structure in your mind's eye? Would you picture the rooms with new colours and textures on the walls and floors; imagine the fixtures and fittings; envision the furnishings and finishing touches? Would you allow the idea of a fresh new look to excite and motivate you?

When I daydream I focus with the end in mind.

Daydreaming is not a time for troubleshooting or worrying. I don't use it as a place to escape from reality but rather a place to create my own. I don't worry about *how* I'm going to achieve what I want, I just focus on *why* I want it. I see the finished product in my mind and feel the excitement and happiness that the attainment of my dream will bring. Daydreaming about overseas travel eventually motivated me to follow my first, simple yet effective, financial plan.

Spin out

Too late I realised I'd braked too suddenly as I felt the car pull sharply to one side. The car went into a spin and I let go of the steering wheel, feeling shocked that the car was now completely out of my control. For the second time in my life I wondered if I was going to die.

It was dusk and I had been travelling along a country road when a kangaroo jumped across into the path of my car. With the car spinning fast I was terrified it would slam into oncoming traffic. I prayed 'Oh God! Please let the road be clear'. Eventually, the car lost momentum and veered backwards off the road and ended up in a ditch. I found myself gazing up at the darkening sky, amazed that I was still alive.

Unbelievably, two men from the NSW Voluntary Rescue Association happened to be driving by as I scrambled up the embankment. It was the early '80s, before mobile phones, so they used their CB radio to call for a tow truck.

The police arrived and because of the angle my car was facing, it was necessary to stop the traffic in both directions in order to pull it back onto the road. It was completely dark now and the flashing lights of police cars and tow trucks pierced the blackness of the surrounding countryside.

Suddenly there was a loud crash, followed closely by a succession of smaller ones. A car had run up the back of the line of waiting cars. No one was injured but several of the cars were wrecked and five of the cars had to be towed away. The bizarre thing was that my car was still drivable.

What followed seemed a bit surreal: people standing by the road looking as numb as I felt; the police directing traffic; cars being hooked up to tow trucks. The VRA guys helped organise people who needed a lift to Sydney and they suggested that we first congregate in a nearby town at a café before we continued on the journey.

This was a great idea; something to calm our frazzled nerves. Some people seemed frustrated, trying to piece together what had happened. As we sat in the little café it gave everyone a chance to unwind and review the events of the evening. I sat sipping tea, which was kind of funny because I didn't normally drink tea. It was warm and soothing and I held the cup like it was an old friend.

Still feeling dazed I sat in a trance-like state until I noticed one of the women was raising her voice, expressing her annoyance at the whole situation. She was indignant. "My car is written off all because **she** hit a kangaroo … and her car is still drivable!" She was clearly annoyed and gestured in my direction as she spoke. I vaguely remember someone springing to my defence, saying, "She couldn't help it if a kangaroo jumped in front of her car." I didn't pay a lot of attention to the conversation after that. All I could think about was how lucky I was to be alive.

It struck me that this woman was feeling so hard done by and yet I felt so blessed. I felt enormous appreciation for those who had helped me.

A lucky attitude

On this occasion it never occurred to me to feel unlucky but there have been times since then when I've felt like things have been out of my control and I've felt unlucky or hard done by. I've had to remind myself that I always have a choice in the way I think and also in how I act and react.

Luck is in the mind of the perceiver. When you think you're lucky you feel good, and if you believe you're unlucky, you feel bad and are more likely to continue to find things that make you feel unlucky. Some people will tell you that they are optimistic and yet complain as soon as something goes wrong.

A lucky attitude comes from thinking of how things could have been worse and discovering the upside of a situation. Looking for things to appreciate enables us remain buoyant or, better still, become uplifted and it is from this platform that we achieve our best results.

The value in comparison and contrast

One day I was having a whinge to my grandmother and she surprised me with her response. *"Oh, you're not so hard done by. Think about children in the world who are worse off than you."* I don't even remember what I was complaining about but her words hit home. I knew there were plenty of kids around the world who didn't have the opportunities that I did.

When I observe others who have less than me I am grateful for what I have. I enjoy inspiring others to improve their situation. When I observe others who are experiencing greater success than me, I appreciate the model they are presenting as it raises the bar.

There is value in comparison when we improve our lives by learning from each other. *I never knew I wanted to travel overseas until I spoke to others who had already done so.* It is natural to seek improvement in any area of our lives. When we thrive we stimulate desire in others. And from this our world becomes a more vibrant and interesting place to live.

Our power is in the present moment

The present is where our power is. Looking back on negative experiences and memories from our past only keeps us in darkness.

Whatever has happened in your past is affecting your present only to the extent that you focus on it. You can't change your past but the way you look back affects who you are. Your ability to reflect on positive experiences from your past will empower you to build the right emotional framework for attracting more things and experiences that are desirable to you. You may not be able to jump from miserable to wonderful at the click of a finger but you can improve the way you feel *right now* by *choosing* to change the way you view things and focusing on things you value in your life.

If you look for misery and hopelessness, you'll find it. If you look for promise and potential, you'll find it. When we choose to focus on things we appreciate, we lift our spirits and find more things to feel good about. When we feel bad, we are a burden to others. When we feel good, we are a pleasure to be around.

You can choose right now how you view your world. Are you in the habit of looking for things to appreciate?

The impact of attitude

As I recognised how powerfully my attitude impacted on the outcomes I got I also noticed when I got on a roll of good luck everything seemed to go right. But when I became frustrated or worried, life became a chore. This realisation helped me to understand why we tend to create positive or negative cycles. Our feelings feed our thoughts which, in turn, affect our outcomes, and those are often what we base our expectations on. Good feelings produce happy positive thoughts, which give more positive reinforcement for great expectations, thereby leading towards positive outcomes.

An individual's attitude and perspective impacts enormously on the world they create around them.

When we appreciate the good things in our life and continue to find a positive slant on situations, no matter who we are with, and no matter what our circumstances are, we view our world from the best possible vantage point.

Look for reasons to feel good

Life is like a treasure hunt, laced with clues for our happiness and wellbeing. Sometimes we are swayed by the beliefs and expectations of others and these can cloud the vision of the person we really want to be. We get distracted or become confused about what is important.

Sometimes I have stumbled along making mistakes, but my ability to bounce back leaves me ready to learn at the next turn. When you're feeling down no one can *make* you feel better. The feeling has to come from within. Even when things are not to our liking, there is always an opportunity for change, for improvement, always room for a shift in perspective or a new way of looking at things.

There have been times when I have taken myself way too seriously. When I remember to lighten up, have fun and find plenty of reasons to laugh, optimism comes more easily to me. When I look for reasons to feel good it becomes easier to embrace the visions of my imagination without limitation.

> **Adopt an attitude that does not recognise failure but instead only looks for evidence of success.**
> - *Make a list of three people who you really appreciate*
> - *Write down three good things that have happened to you today or this week. Savour the feeling you get when you focus on experiences you have enjoyed and imagine more good things coming your way.*
> - *Lighten up, have some fun and find plenty of reasons to laugh.*

Develop habits that will feed your optimism

It is easy to look at someone's success and feel optimistic just as it is easy to look at failure and feel pessimistic. Become incurably optimistic by regularly identifying people, places and things in your day-to-day life that you appreciate.

Some may think that it would be glorious to be positive 100 per cent of the time, but that would become monotonous. The thrills in our life come when we relish the natural curiosity we are born with, which prompts us to continue to explore the variety of our surroundings.

In our pursuit of diversity, we continue to experience contrast; we experiment and make mistakes, get some things wrong and some things right. And when you become incurably optimistic for long enough, things go right, often in a serendipitous sequence of events, and then you realise that you have achieved something you have dreamed about!

Our best results come out of our passion rather than purely our labours. For me, travelling the world extensively by age 23 was huge. I experienced so much diversity I eventually craved stability and came home.

After we have achieved a dream life has a tendency to return to normality. If you're like me, sooner or later you'll want more contrast. If you don't get enough diversity, you get bored; too much and you can become overwhelmed by the choices the contrast brings and eventually crave some stability. What a wonderful cycle! For me, it's what makes life fun.

Following my overseas adventures, new dreams fuelled my thirst for life, and more surprises lay ahead. My treasure hunt was soon to broaden to a place where I had more people to organise than just myself and my propensity towards optimism was to be tested like never before.

5

Lucky links

Becoming aware of the potential in those around you

Lucky people build and maintain a strong 'network of luck'
From *The Luck Factor* by Dr Richard Wiseman

Grey daze

It was raining again. It seemed like it had been raining forever. The weather was getting cold and when I pulled some of my winter shoes from their boxes at the bottom of the wardrobe they were coated in mould.

My life had changed considerably from one of the party girl of several years before. I was married with two children, both under two years of age. My husband and I had bought a small house and taken on a big mortgage. Interest rates back then were around 18 per cent. We were now living on one income and money was tight.

Being a mother was a mysterious new role. I felt that my children had been sent from heaven to me and I felt blessed to have them, but was baffled at how other mothers seemed to get so much done and managed to be so organised.

Not having much of a clue about motherhood, I was glad to have a mother-in-law who was supportive and helpful. She suggested that little children often respond well to a routine. I followed her advice and found it did help me to feel more in control.

But the grey weather continued on and just about every time I planned to go out for a walk, it would start drizzling. I'd think about going for a drive and it would begin to pour. Our garage was down the back of the block and very narrow so I had to manoeuvre one child into the car at a time. Some days when the rain was coming down it all seemed too hard, so I would stay at home in our little house watching the water run down the window panes. I had a great deal to be grateful for and yet I began to feel a bit like my shoes: cooped up and mouldy.

Seven people a day

Following months on end of rainy weather, I paid a routine visit to the local baby health clinic. After giving the baby a clean bill of health, the nurse, Jan, turned her attention to me. She seemed to sense my grey mood and asked how I was. I told her I was fine. But she looked at me a little longer and asked me again. "How are you, really?" I admitted I felt low and I couldn't understand why.

It was a relief to talk to her about how I felt. It wasn't something that I would have thought to discuss with anyone else. Being a ridiculously optimistic person, I did not normally allow myself to admit that things weren't right.

My chat with Jan highlighted the fact that I had been lurking around the house too many days without enough social interaction. I had friends and family I could visit but I had slipped into the habit of spending a great deal of time with limited adult company. Jan gave me some advice that day and what she said has stuck in my mind ever since: *"You need seven people a day for mental health".*

This made perfect sense. I had felt restricted by a lack of money as well as the weather. I decided to look for outings and activities, either free or low cost, which would get the three of us out of the house and among other people, in any weather. I ramped up contact with a local mothers' group and joined a playgroup as well.

Within a few weeks, I was offered weekend work waitressing for a caterer. It turned out to be fun because I was working at weddings and functions where I was waiting on people who were in party mode. My spirits began to lift. I really enjoyed my new job as it helped me to reclaim my identity. For a few hours a week I was being Julie again. Not mum or housewife … just me. And I vowed there would be no more lonely rainy days—even if it meant getting drenched I was determined to see at least seven different smiles every day!

A timely gift

Going from insular to integrated, I made an effort to contact old friends. Katrina, a former work colleague, came to visit. We had become good friends as we spent many lunch hours together running, swimming or just strolling through Sydney's Botanic Gardens. She was a happy girl with a contagious laugh and she seemed to have a knack of being in the right place at the right time.

We chatted over dinner and promised to keep in touch. Within a week she was true to her word. She called me and said she wanted to drop around as she had something for me. It was a book by Andrew Matthews called *Being Happy*. Typically of Katrina, the book turned out to be the right gift at the right time. It was just the thing to lift my spirits.

The magnetic power of the mind

Having filled my head for years with various genres of fiction, I was not in the habit of reading self-help books. So this book was completely different to anything I had ever read. I felt like little light globes were being switched on inside my head. I instantly recognised some of the less useful patterns I had fallen into and also recognised these in others. I laughed when I saw Matthews' little cartoons of people who whinge about their poor state of health or sad lot in life. I was intrigued by the magnetic power of the mind.

"Your mind is a magnet and you attract what you think about."

This statement leapt off the page at me. The concept of our thoughts acting like magnets was fascinating to me as I began to see evidence of it in many areas of my life. I could see how I had attracted many good things but also some less desirable aspects. I realised how my attention to the gloomy weather had affected my mood.

I experimented with affirmations and changed the way I spoke to my kids. Instead of yelling warnings, I gave clearer (and somewhat calmer) directions of what I wanted them to do. For example, simple things like *'Don't leave things lying around'* became *'Put your things away when you've finished with them'*. I focused on what I wanted rather than telling them what I didn't want. It was glaringly obvious and yet something I noticed that other parents sometimes failed to recognise.

> A decision to deliberately direct your thoughts can impact enormously on your ability to attract the things you want

It applies to the way we express what we want from others and also how we speak to ourselves (our self-talk). It is often not until we recognise some of our negative self-talk that we make a decision to replace it with more positive self-directives.

At this point in my life, I was much more interested in being happy than attracting money so my immediate focus was to strengthen my self-confidence. I knew that my happiness was up to me. I couldn't expect anyone else to *make* me happy. I had to find it within myself.

I realised that I had developed some negative thought patterns and laughed when I read Matthews' descriptions of positive thought patterns. He gave examples of people who are always affirming their good health, their prosperity or their good luck. I thought of people I knew who did this and wondered, *Could something so simple really make a difference?*

While I was writing this book, a woman challenged me on the subject matter. She couldn't understand why I wanted to write about happiness. She thought I should stick to writing about making money because she assumed that having money makes people happy. But having money is not an assurance of happiness and I'm so glad that I had the sense to come to this **_knowing_** before I set out to make money. Happiness happens in your head and in your heart before it appears in your life. Money is the same. What this woman didn't understand is that these lessons apply to all the things we want. Health, wealth and happiness; when you get your thinking right, you can have it all.

Making a deliberate decision to direct my thoughts challenged my tendency towards impatience. I was hungry for radical change. I wanted *it* all NOW. But I noticed that even small changes in my thinking held value. Developing a more optimistic pattern of thought was enough to tip the balance in the right direction. I had to train myself to be happy with small improvements and trust that it was setting the stage for things that were to come. Now, with the benefit of hindsight, I know that *any* improvement in the way you feel is a step in the right direction.

Learning about the power of the mind confirmed my suspicion that I could choose to have a great deal more control over my life than I had previously believed. Our attracting power is in our focus. Repeated patterns of positive thoughts bring good results.

Lucky links

Having realised the value in seeing at least seven people day, I wanted to maximise the impact of that by linking up with more people who were upbeat and easy to be around. I wanted to be happy more of the time, and figured my chances of being cheerful and fortunate were greatly increased if I hung around with other happy and successful people. People who treat everyone they meet with the same respect. My Dad is like this. You could be the queen or the cleaner and he will offer the same level of esteem.

Our ability to feel happy hinges enormously on the quality of the relationships we foster. I was coming to understand that my relationship with myself was the most important because nothing will strain a relationship more than an expectation that someone else should make you happy. Being truly happy with *who you are* is the ultimate freedom.

A new concept was forming in my mind: people I thought of as *lucky links*. *Lucky links* are people, like my friend Katrina, who inspire you, laugh with you and encourage you. They are people who are happy *whether or not you are happy*. They are people who find reasons to be happy no matter who they are with and no matter what they, or others, are doing.

To find *lucky links* I had to learn to be one myself and with more major changes on the way, life was about to provide me with greater challenge and new opportunities to test my theories.

New kid on the block

"Oh, she'll probably be here soon," she said with an offhand wave as she gestured toward the empty doorway. She turned back to her conversation, leaving me with no hint of a welcome or introduction to the other women. I felt suddenly excluded and alone.

When I'd agreed to move to Canberra because my husband was offered a job there, it was not a decision I put a lot of thought into. My husband saw it as a way of escaping our big Sydney mortgage. The trouble was it didn't occur to me just how much I would miss the big city excitement.

Wanting to make friends quickly, I joined a tennis group at which I met a lady called Brenda. She invited me to a playgroup she attended with her children. She told me the time and place and we arranged to meet there. But Brenda was late and I was standing waiting. Being ignored made me feel like an unwelcome outsider and caused me to feel unusually shy. I had imagined that people would go out of their way to make me feel welcome. But no one invited me or my kids to join in. We just stood around waiting for Brenda to show up.

Over half an hour later Brenda appeared with a casual smile. She apologised for being late and introduced me to the others. I remember that first half an hour seemed like a very long time. I felt resentful that the women had not been friendly enough to include me in on their conversations. Even after the introductions they were a little cool and I wished I had not bothered. Being the new kid on the block was not as easy as I'd thought it would be. My lucky links were thin on the ground and for a while I felt lonely and vulnerable.

A network of luck

Missing my Sydney friends made me determined to make new ones. Eventually I befriended a group of mothers at the pre-school my daughter attended. We became close friends and as we began to hang out more together my husband dubbed us *The Rat Pack*.

All packs seem to have a natural leader and ours was named *Queen Rat*. Although I had arrived on the scene months ahead of her, she had made many more new friends and contacts than I had. I asked her secret. She told me that her husband had been in the army and she had moved with her family a number of times before. She found the best thing to do was to throw herself headlong into things. She would enrol the kids in school and then sign them up for some extra-curricular stuff like sport or music. She would then join a couple of different groups herself.

Queen Rat explained that these extra commitments had two benefits. Firstly they kept everyone busy so they had less time to miss friends they had left behind. Secondly they maximised their interaction with others and made it more likely that they would make new friends more quickly. *Queen Rat* knew the immense value in friendship and of surrounding yourself with lucky links. She was building and maintaining a network of luck.

Though her strategy seemed glaringly obvious, there was something else *Queen Rat* had going for her that earned her the title of queen. It was something I had neglected to do the day I went to the playgroup. *Queen Rat* greeted people with a big smile, wide eyes and unbridled enthusiasm. She engaged people in conversation by asking them questions about themselves. I wonder how differently that first half hour of playgroup would have gone if I'd arrived wearing my best smile instead of allowing myself to slip into shyness and insecurity. Ever since the playgroup experience, I have endeavoured to make an effort to welcome newcomers to a group knowing what it is like to be in their shoes.

Positive and negative connections

Our interactions with others can cause us to feel the whole gamut of emotions ... some good, some bad. When I didn't know any better, I sometimes blamed others for the way I felt. I wasn't always prepared to take responsibility for my emotions.

Negative interactions are an opportunity for us to identify what we don't like in a relationship. The contrast, the good and bad we perceive in others, gives us an opportunity to recognise what we do like. I didn't like being ignored and left out so I had to work out how I could get the opposite of that. I realised that I can't change the way others behave around me but I can change the way I act and react around them. When I look for and focus on the *positive* attributes of others I am much more likely to create more *lucky links*.

When we become aware of the magnetic power of the human mind we recognise that we attract what we think about. Thinking *I hate it when people snub me* will only attract more cold shoulders; thinking *I hate it when I feel left out* will only attract more loneliness. The real work in relationships is identifying what **you do like** and focusing **only** on that. If you hate being snubbed think of a time when you have been included and welcomed and **hold on to that feeling**. Imagine yourself enjoying the company of like-minded others. What is drawing others to you and you to them?

How do you greet your world?

In order to get seven smiles, you first have to give them. In order to get seven great conversations, you have to be prepared to take an interest in others and allow them to take an interest in you. People reflect back at you what you are projecting from within but what shows on the surface also has an impact.

Imagine you are about to greet someone, anyone. It could be the queen or the cleaner. If a mirror were to suddenly appear before your face what would you see? How do you greet the world?

> An ability to make favourable impressions on others can open many doors.

I have met people who have lots of money but are not very happy, so I know that money can't buy happiness. That is why my quest is to help people to achieve both greater happiness **and** prosperity.

Like everyone, I've had frustrating and challenging times in my life when the last thing I've felt like doing is smiling, but now I ask myself: *How long am I prepared to stay miserable? If I look hard enough I'll find someone to feed my sorrow, someone who will listen to my woes and recount theirs to me.* But what am I attracting when I focus on things I don't want? *Lucky links* are people who uplift you and bring out the best in you and in order to find *lucky links* you need to become that to others.

Some of my favourite *lucky links* are great at linking people together. They throw wonderful parties and seem to have a never-ending source of useful contacts.

Lucky links give us something to admire: they may be friendly, clever, helpful and charismatic; they may be socially adept or possess an uncanny ability to turn the tides of good fortune in their favour. **Whatever you have admired in another, you have the potential to be yourself**.

Sliver of pie

"It's a workshop on abundance," she declared. My friend, one of my new lucky links, was working for a local psychologist. She invited me, and several others, to attend a workshop run by her employer. I didn't normally attend workshops, but the theme of abundance had me intrigued so I decided to go along.

The psychologist spoke about appreciation and being aware of what we already have that we are thankful for. She also discussed perceptions, how people can have different reactions to, and perceptions of, the same or similar experience. She talked of beliefs and how people make judgements without knowing all the facts.

She gave the example of an audience giving a standing ovation at the end of a concert. One person is sitting down. What did it mean? We all jumped in with various reasons why the person was still sitting when *everyone else was standing. These included things like "they didn't like the concert", "they had a broken leg" and so on.*

The psychologist waited patiently while we exhausted every possible option. She then repeated the question, "What did it mean that this person was still seated?" She told us this in itself didn't mean anything. We were making judgements and assumptions without knowing all the facts.

She turned to the whiteboard and drew a circle. She asked the group questions about how people obtain income. Someone suggested that many people work for a wage or salary. She agreed and asked for more ideas.

The group came up with a variety of ways a person could obtain an income. They included profits or dividends from business or investments, welfare, lottery or prize winnings, charity, inheritance, gifts, allowances and proceeds from criminal activity.

Then she asked questions aimed at dividing the population into categories of how much (perceived) effort was involved in obtaining different-sized incomes. For example:

- *Some people work hard and don't earn much money*
- *Some people work hard and earn an average income*
- *Some people work hard and earn a lot of money*
- *Some people don't work very hard (or not at all) and have a small income*

Finally, when we thought we had exhausted all the options, the psychologist asked us, "Do you think there are people who don't work hard at all yet make a lot of money?"

The group agreed that there were people who would fit into this group, but it would be a very small group indeed. In fact, as she divided the circle into segments, this group was represented by the smallest sliver of pie.

As the group sat and discussed which piece of pie they would fit into, a little light came on in my head. I knew exactly which group I wanted to fit into. It was the tiniest sliver of all.

Sometimes our lucky links take us places we wouldn't normally go. This episode stretched my mind and rekindled my interest in psychology. I liked the way the psychologist drew our attention to facts with an absence of judgement. She helped clear the muddy waters of my mind that had been clouded with beliefs and assumptions based on my perceptions. It made me consider that assumptions and beliefs are often flawed because perceptions can be deceptive. **A perception is only a point of view at a point in time.**

From my own experience I could see why people made assumptions about money that were based on probabilities rather than possibilities. I vowed to open my mind up to new possibilities. If there was a way to make a lot of money without having to work very hard, I was determined to find it.

The world is full of lucky links

Eventually I came to the conclusion that everyone we come into contact with has the potential to be a *lucky link*, whether they are clever and socially adept or not. Everyone has something to offer. Some people serve as role models and others make us acutely aware of what we don't want, which in turn offers additional clues to our own success. When we focus on positive interactions and consider the benefits of our connections with the fascinating people we mix with, we are more likely to find more *lucky links*.

Since I came up with the idea of *lucky links* I have vastly improved my ability to make strong positive connections with people. It doesn't mean that I like everyone I meet, but when I meet people I do like, I can bond with them quickly. This has had a huge positive impact on both my professional and personal life.

The concept of *lucky links* and how it relates to your ability to make money is expanded upon throughout the rest of the book.

Seven smiles

There is always someone worse off than you, maybe someone you can help or someone whose lack can help you appreciate what you have. Likewise, there is always someone better off than you, someone to give you hope, someone who will encourage and inspire you to strive for happiness and more of life's joys. With over 6 billion people on the planet, there is endless opportunity to find yourself some *lucky links* and the best way to get seven smiles is to smile more at people you meet.

Lucky links were opening doors in my mind and leading me to new opportunities. But again my life was about to undergo another major change and my ability to adapt was to be tested like never before.

Reinvention

Creating a new identity for yourself

If you want things to be different, perhaps the answer is to become different yourself.

Norman Vincent Peale

Fear of change

A teardrop trickled down my face and fell into my cup of tea. I half laughed through my tears at what a miserable soul I had become. I was sitting at a friend's kitchen bench crying because I felt trapped. I wanted the best for my children, but felt my choices were limited. A big decision like divorce would rock their world but I knew that avoiding change was making me shrink inside.

For months I'd put myself under enormous emotional self-scrutiny, feeling I was stuck between a rock and a hard place. To cope with the stress that was burgeoning within, I found relief in hefty serves of physical exertion. I was playing social and competition tennis and this seemed to help, so I added to my exercise routine by walking up a nearby mountain. The walk took me over two hours from my house, but as I got fitter I became quicker and this allowed me more time at the top.

I'd sit on a rock at the peak and gaze out across the city, wondering what life had in store for me. No matter how dejected I felt when I set out from the base of the mountain I always felt my spirits lifted considerably by the time I reached the top.

But keeping my worries bottled up was like having a virus eating away at my insides. My sprints up the mountain seemed to build my inner strength and eventually I relaxed enough to allow myself to confide in a close friend, who did what any good friend would do. She made me tea and listened as I unloaded my troubles and cried into my cup.

Our interaction that day reminded me of the enormous value of talking to others to gain another perspective on a problem. My friend encouraged me to seek other opinions. She suggested I go to a counsellor. At first I rejected this idea but with no better options in my mind at the time, I decided to give it a go. The counsellor asked me a question that challenged my thinking. He asked what I would be teaching my children about relationships if I stayed in one that I was not happy in.

It dawned on me that my choice was between expansion or contraction, and even though both scared me I knew I wanted my kids to live a life full of options and opportunity. I didn't want them to see me stuck, afraid to make a move. With the help of the counsellor and a few close friends, my fear of shrinking became overwritten by a growing hopefulness at the prospect of reinventing myself.

How much do you want change?

If you want to effect some positive change in your life then this story is of great relevance. No matter whether you want to achieve a sizeable shift in your prosperity or whether you want improved or new relationships, the principles are the same.

Imagine you decided to tell some of your friends and family that you are sick of not having enough money and you are ready to make your fortune this year. How do you think others would respond to your intention? In a perfect world, everyone you tell would be supportive and wish you well in your ventures. But it is possible that some would take it upon themself to enlighten you as to the probabilities of your success, based on what they perceive you are capable of? Some may even consider your desires greedy or selfish. But who are they to judge?

When I told several close friends and family members of my doubts about my marriage, they were supportive and understanding. But once I'd made the decision and the news went around, things changed. One girlfriend warned me, *"Julie, you'd better be prepared for other people's reactions. Some just won't understand why you are leaving a nice guy. It would be different if he was a bastard."* My friend was right. My husband was a nice guy and some people just didn't understand.

The sad irony was that the girlfriend who said this to me stayed with her husband. I found out a couple of years later that he was beating her. I was so surprised because she seemed like such a strong person. I couldn't understand why she stayed with him.

Liberating or restrictive thinking

The prospect of significant change can be a source of fear or excitement. It is a strange irony that a life-changing event can seem so scary and yet be so liberating. I had been so concerned about the possible negative consequences of divorce on my kids that, for a while, I couldn't imagine the benefits. Divorce, like any life-changing event, can be a restrictive or liberating experience. It depends how you approach it and who you choose to listen to.

It is easy to get fixed views on a subject by listening to what society feeds us. I had been fed negative views on the subject of separation and divorce and it wasn't until I opened my mind up to the benefits it could hold that I changed my view. When we separated, my ex-husband and I made a pact to work towards positive outcomes for our kids. This attitude has had ongoing benefits for us all.

Listening to helpful ideas from others enabled me to shift from feeling restricted, thinking that my options were limited, to being more open-minded and realising that the positive options were more extensive than I had considered. But I had to ignore the negative reactions of others in order to maintain my resolve and continue with my reinvention.

It is possible to become so used to feelings of frustration or discontent that you learn to live with them. I've met people who blame their partner, their job or the economy for their lack of freedom yet the thing that could set them free is to change their thinking. Many assume that to become liberated they need to change their situation but restriction or liberation happens in your head before it appears in your life.

Decision brings relief from procrastination

Going through a divorce was not an ugly or bitter experience but it was sad. We all took time to adapt to the changes. But making a decision to effect significant change gave me relief from the agony of my procrastination. Thinking that being selfless was the answer, I had been denying myself and while I did this I had less to offer those that I loved. When I began to change my thinking, it allowed me to overcome my fear and edge my way towards hope. With each new step I felt my resilience rising up from within. Fear had held me back and kept me in limbo, in a place where I felt I was going nowhere fast—a place that stunted my personal growth. When I released myself from the struggle of indecision, I became increasingly motivated to explore new possibilities.

Whether we go searching for it or not, change is inevitable. Relationships change because people change. The emotionally charged experience of divorce, like any major change in your life, can provide the opportunity to undergo a huge reinvention.

Avoiding change can leave us wallowing in procrastination, going from one insignificant choice to another as we search for relief. But the avoidance only prolongs our fear. People who learn to become adaptable and flexible in their attitude towards life tend to be excited by change and look for the opportunities it presents.

Making the decision to embrace change gave me enormous relief. **The prospect of significant change presents us with a choice of being ruled by fear or fuelled by excitement.** And shifting from fear to excitement can happen quite quickly once you stop fighting the fear and begin **expecting** something better.

A roller-coaster of change

"Don't worry about her. She's like that with everyone." A bright-eyed dark-haired girl stood in the doorway to my office. She introduced herself as Mandy and I felt comfortable with her straight away. Mandy had a light-hearted disposition and a mischievous look in her eye that made me suspect we would become friends.

The woman Mandy had been referring to was our surly supervisor, who had just left my office leaving me feeling overwhelmed. As part of my reinvention, I had rejoined the workforce and this was my first day back in an office job after more than five years. I felt nervous and insecure about my outdated office skills. With new computer technology to wrap my head around, and a gruff supervisor to deal with, my self-confidence had slipped.

Mandy's smile was reassuring. Although she had only started a couple of days before me, she had been temping for years and was comfortable with the challenge of quickly familiarising herself with a new office environment. She sat with me and patiently explained several idiosyncrasies of the computer system. My confidence began to resurface. I was determined to function at a pace that would motivate the employer to extend my contract.

Find friends who feed your feelings of freedom

It turned out that Mandy, and two other girls in the office, had all been recently divorced. These three women, the terrific trio, did wonders to lift my self-confidence and reassured me that there was definitely a promise of a good life for me and a bright future for my children. The four of us became good friends and they inspired me to lighten up and have some fun.

We frequented the pub too often, drank too much, swore way more than necessary and laughed very loudly at the slightest hiccup. Partying with these women helped me regain my feeling of invincibility and life became a lot more exciting.

Once I'd hopped onto the roller-coaster of change, my life began to take unexpected twists and turns. Among the challenges I faced in regaining my independence came a few pleasant surprises—not the least of which was the discovery that I still held appeal to the opposite sex. The terrific trio laughed at me when I was taken aback by the flirtations of several male work colleagues. It hadn't occurred to me that my now very fit body, which had been hidden under tracksuits for several years, would attract much attention.

Born-again woman

Adjusting to single life with two young children and a mortgage of my very own was a memorable point in my life. Although I was still doing temp work, I was happy to be earning money of my own and learning new things. But people around me were encouraging me to get a safe, secure job so I would have more stability in my life. Safety, security and stability were not things I had been giving a great deal of thought to, but when enough people tell you something, you begin to think it must be the truth.

Following the advice of these well-meaning loved ones, I took on a longer assignment. The person who had previously filled the role had done regular overtime. I made it clear when I accepted the position that overtime and me didn't agree. My kids were my priority and I was determined to work quickly and efficiently all day in order to leave at five and head home to be with them.

At the time, I was also taking saxophone lessons, playing in a concert band and studying for my third grade AMEB[2] saxophone examination. My boss was a career-oriented lady, also in her thirties. She didn't have any children and was fascinated by my ability to master my time and juggle so many priorities. Observing my re-emergence into a full-time, long-term assignment while being a mum, running a household, being a musician and conducting a relatively active social life, she dubbed me a "born-again woman".

The time management skills I was developing in my new job became crucial to the running of my increasingly busy life. I played my saxophone in the park across the road from the office in my lunch break and studied music theory at night when the kids went to sleep. When I spoke to

---

2 Australian Music Examinations Board

people about all the things I was doing, they seemed so impressed. "How do you do it? You're like superwoman!"

When enough people comment on your ability to do something well you begin to believe them and you think it must be the truth. Being busy was making me feel very capable. Feeling capable was very nice. It made me feel important so I wallowed in the feeling for as long as I could. But much as I wanted to cling to my newfound importance, I began to wonder if this busy, safe, secure existence was for me.

I was spending time pleasing others and doing what I thought would impress the rest of the world and yet spending very little time with myself. Being a born-again woman was not as glamorous as it had first sounded.

Exploring extremes to find balance

The *born-again woman* I had become was in stark contrast to the girl who had felt cooped up and mouldy several years earlier. But we often regain our balance by first exploring the extremes. I went from having not enough people, to having so many interactions that I had no time to myself. I'd also gone from not having very much money, to having more money but less time. It was yet to occur to me how I could have plenty of money *and* control over my time.

During this time of significant change, my happiness was imperative. I was not interested in *making* money. I just wanted enough to enjoy life with my kids. I wanted to focus on one thing at a time. Happiness first; the big money could wait.

The serial dater

Being single again was scary at first. Once I got over the shock and met women like the terrific trio, who had not only survived divorce but were thriving, I realised that being single could be a lot of fun. I was still a devoted mother and homemaker but when my kids went to their Dad's I transformed into party girl.

Together with my friends, I frequented nightclubs and bars and attended parties, and my social life blossomed. Single men abounded and over the next couple of years I dated a string of interesting, friendly, funny and good-looking men.

Although I was having a great deal of fun, the single-again novelty began to wear off. I'd reinvented myself as someone who was strong, capable and independent, and a bit of a party animal, but I felt like something was missing.

For a while I thought finding a new man would complete my picture. I was meeting the sort of guys you could introduce to your family and friends and was waiting for the sirens and flashing lights to go off in my head saying **this is the one.** *But the sirens and lights didn't come. When I wasn't out searching I felt a bit lost and lonely. Without realising it I had become a serial dater, hoping Mr Right would come along and make me happy.*

Thinking that some further reinvention might do the trick, I decided to make some more changes in my life. I quit my job and enrolled in pre-tertiary studies at a local technical college. I wanted to get a university degree so people would think I was clever and take me more seriously. But after several weeks at college, I became distracted again. A girl in my class was lead singer with a Latin band and she invited me to bring my sax and join them at practice. I was beginning to wonder if I was just a fun magnet as I found playing in bands much more interesting than what I was learning at college.

The prospect of years of study made me feel constricted, so I quit college and got a part-time job. It occurred to me that going to university just so others would think I was clever was not such a bright idea. How I felt about myself was becoming more important than what others thought about me.

The road to reinvention

These experiences held many lessons for me. I have since learned to embrace the unpredictability of my nature. Sometimes I commit to things and other times I flit about on the winds of change like a butterfly, hungry for adventure. And it is the variety of life that fuels my fire. If I try to engage in an activity that is boring to me I get distracted and end up going off on a tangent anyway.

Pursuing diversity provides more opportunity to refine what you want. If you think of life as a smorgasbord, it's really up to you how much choice you want. Would you rather choose from a small selection of food or would you like a full-on banquet? There is no right or wrong answer to this question but I have found that the more I pursue diversity, the wider my choices. With greater choice I was exposed to more opportunity, and with increased opportunity I found more ways to enjoy life and have fun!

Filling the void

When I was feeling like something was missing, what I really wanted was to be happy with myself. For a while I thought that happiness relied on exterior circumstances but now I know that it comes from our own perception. The way to fill the void is to find reasons to feel happy by looking for things to appreciate. The answer is simple yet elusive because of the complexity of our lives. Sometimes we are so focused on what is missing in our life we forget to be glad about things or people we already have.

When I cared more about how I felt and worried less about what others thought, I freed myself up to do things that I loved. Working part-time meant I could spend more time with my kids and this made me feel *much* happier. Even though this meant I was earning less money, I was happy to have more time to consider what was important to me.

As I took time to appreciate the wonderful things in my life I became less inclined to try to impress others. If people found me interesting I wanted it to happen naturally. I wanted to be true to myself rather than trying to be what I thought society expected of me. I felt satisfied with my life in a way that I hadn't expected. I spent more quality time with my kids and, when I was alone, I was more contented in my own company. I felt less compelled to rush out and party at any opportunity. Being a serial dater had been fun, but what was more fun was feeling really good about me.

The secret to happiness

Some people seem to think that one day they'll discover the secret to happiness and then they will live happily ever after. But where would be the fun in that? Since this time I have found millions of other things that irritate me but as I have overcome each one, I have strengthened my resilience and my ability to quickly regain an optimistic standpoint. With each triumph, no matter how seemingly significant or insignificant, I become stronger and life gets better. With each new irony, my sense of humour broadens and I laugh more.

Little children know the secret to happiness. It's like we are born with a ***knowing*** yet, for some strange reason, we forget. We forget to appreciate the positive aspects of our life; to be happy in the moment. We forget that it is normal to thrive, natural to love, invigorating to laugh as spontaneously and as often as possible. We forget that it is okay to become bored and crave more diversity, more affluence, more toys to play with and more excitement.

Love is like a magnet

When I was looking for Mr Right to make me happy I was forgetting to love myself and the people I already had in my life. The love I was seeking was readily available but I couldn't find it while I was busy perceiving lack. I was so busy noticing that I didn't have a man to love that I sometimes forgot to fully appreciate the people who already loved me.

> *To find the love **of** your life, find the love **in** your life.*

We don't find love when we are lonely, we find love when we are *loving*. Our world is full of people, places and things that we can admire and love. When I began to spend more time appreciating the love in my life, I realised that love is like a magnet. By focusing on the love we have we are bound to attract more. When I was feeling lonely and wishing I had a man to love I was focusing on lack. When I allowed Mr Right to take shape in my mind and *trusted* that he would eventually appear, it was easier for me to relax and appreciate the love I already had around me.

Improve your ability to cope with change
- *Make more decisions. Avoid the agony of procrastination by making a decision to effect change. Even small decisions open up your options.*
- *Pursue diversity in order to broaden your choices, exposing you to greater opportunity and enjoyment of life*
- *Rekindle the little child within you who remembers what it takes to be happy*
- *Appreciate the positive aspects of your life RIGHT NOW*
- **Continue** *to look for reasons to feel good*

7

Serendipity

**Listening to your inner voice
and honing your instincts**

"That dress looks great, but change your shoes, put on some make-up and fix your hair. You never know who you might meet tonight." My friend Caroline had come to pick me up. It was our friend Paula's birthday and we were going to her house for dinner.

It was kind of funny that Caroline was bossing me around telling me how to look. She didn't normally talk that way. And I didn't really know what the big deal was. We were only going to Paula's house. We weren't planning on going 'out on the town'. But Caroline sounded so convincing that I marched back down the hallway to the bathroom. We chatted as I painted my face, adorned myself with jewellery, fixed my hair and shoved my feet into some silly shiny stilettos. "How's that?" I asked as I turned to Caroline for the final inspection. "Much better!" she declared. "Let's go."

We arrived at Paula's to find a surprise guest thrown into the mix. Paula's friend Andrew seemed eager for a good time, and the dinner conversation was animated. After dinner, Andrew suggested we go to a local club where there was a band playing. He said he'd heard the band was good and would probably draw a big crowd.

Having finally overcome my serial dating compulsion, I was happy sipping wine and chatting at Paula's table. I'd come out with a simple expectation of enjoying the company of friends but I could see that Andrew was keen for a faster pace. He roused us from our comfortable positions and into the car.

The hunch that packed a punch

"That lead singer sounds divine," I crooned. We'd settled in at the club and were listening to the band when I noticed his voice. It was hypnotic as it filtered through the noise coming from the crowd around my table. I felt mesmerised. I was having fun with my friends but felt compelled to find the voice and see what he looked like.

The place was filling up fast and the dance floor was packed. I'd made my way through the crowd to the stage to get a closer look. Reaching a good vantage point I stood and watched. The band was all male and all were singing, but it only took me a second to figure out which one owned the voice. I could tell by the way he moved.

At my insistence, Paula and Caroline got up from the table to take a closer look. "Yeah, he's alright, I guess," was their casual response. It was obvious he wasn't setting them on fire.

Amid the chatter and laughter, the dulcet tones continued to entice me from across the room. I felt like he was singing just for me. "That's the man of my dreams!" I chirped. My friends laughed and told me to have another drink.

At the end of the set I watched him walk to the bar with a couple of the other band members. It was then that it hit me. I had a strong compulsion to go and talk to him. A part of me was scared and shy but another part of me said, "Just do it, don't think about it—just go and talk to him".

Obeying my inner voice I walked straight up to him and smiled. I gazed at him and told him how much I was enjoying listening to the band. Then I asked him a question. I asked if he made a living out of *music. He told me he did. I was thrilled. It wasn't often I met someone who made their sole living out of music. Conversation just flowed. He was easy to talk to and felt good to be around.*

Months later, when I married him, both Caroline and Paula recalled with fascination my words that evening: "That's the man of my dreams!" They knew I didn't normally talk that way. I'd had hunches before but this one packed a punch!

It has also stuck in my mind what Caroline said to me when she had come to pick me up that evening, "You never know who you might meet."

Chemistry

Since this time dating has changed a bit. Now I have friends who search on the internet for a partner. It may work for some but I'm so pleased that I found my second husband the old-fashioned way. Well, that's if you can call picking someone up in a bar 'old-fashioned'. I'm glad I didn't try and pick someone from a list of attributes or interests because I think I would have passed him by. Apart from music, we didn't seem to have much in common but the *chemistry* was strong and that's not something you can get off a computer screen. It was a serendipitous match that *felt* right from the start.

Trusting your instincts

Following this experience I have developed a huge reverence for my gut feelings because I know that when I pay attention to this inner guidance things go *really well*. It is not something that is easy to explain but the evidence speaks for itself. My second husband, Simon, and I have a lot of fun *and* make money together which enables us to live the lifestyle of our choosing.

Intuition or inner guidance is something we all have available to us. Through the stories that follow, I hope to help you to tune in to yours.

The doom and gloom before the boom

When we met, Simon and I each had an ordinary median level suburban house and a mortgage. Not long after we were married there was a change in federal government. With it came changes in policy and in the months that followed, considerable numbers of government employees were laid off and, being a temp, I was one of the first to go.

Before long the talk of the town was of doom and gloom. People were leaving the city to find work elsewhere and real estate prices dropped. With both our houses worth less than we paid for them, we decided to live in my house and rent out Simon's while we waited for the market to recover.

Despite these setbacks, the doomsayers did not hold my attention for long. It made no sense to gripe about tough times. The slumping real estate market and my job loss were minor glitches. With six children between us, Simon and I were focused on adjusting to our new family formation.

As office jobs were thin on the ground, I decided to do something different. I took a lower paid, lower status job. I didn't think a lot about it. I was simply focused on getting a job and, for the time being, I was prepared to compromise.

Over 13 years on, there has again been talk of doom and gloom. Although, this time on a global scale, it is to me, no different than before. There is *always* opportunity, but if you focus on a perceived lack, then that is what you are likely to experience. As it is human nature to find solutions and search for answers, any period of doom and gloom is simply a lead-up to the next boom.

When people ask me for advice about real estate investing, they often don't realise that I came in the back door. I didn't set out as an 'investor'. Simon and I became investors by default, and the results from our early endeavours were patchy and far from astounding. My motivation for our first two joint property purchases came from a desire for a better home for our family. At the time, I had no idea that investing in real estate would have such a powerfully positive impact on my lifestyle.

A clean slate

"Use your imagination!" she said, as I looked blankly at her. *"Be creative!"* came the next suggestion. She then turned and disappeared back into the shop. I had taken a job working part-time at a busy local pharmacy and my supervisor had asked me to redecorate the display window at the front of the shop. I had stared at her wide-eyed. Serving customers inside the shop was easy, but window-dressing was right outside my box.

This job was far less cushy than what I had become accustomed to in the public service, but it was better than staying at home and feeling sorry for myself. I gazed at the display window that was jam-packed with products. Use my imagination? Be creative? What did that mean? I figured I mustn't be a very imaginative or creative person. I didn't know where to begin.

As I stood and pondered the best way to tackle the project, it eventually occurred to me to start with a clean slate. I pulled the existing display products out and dusted the shelves. Then I stood back and gazed at the empty window. This made all the difference. I now had space to work with. I gathered various gift boxes and appealingly packaged products and arranged them in the window until it was busy again but this time with a different theme. My display was hardly award-winning but I had a feeling that the exercise was to provide an answer that I did not yet have a question for.

Society robots

Within a couple of months I had a call from an agency offering me a government contract. Doom and gloom doesn't last long if you don't give it your attention. The call from the agency came as a surprise. I had become preoccupied enjoying the customer service aspect of the retail sales environment. I found it stimulating to see people getting results all day long; walking into the shop and walking out with what they came in for. The results may seem small or simple compared to running a country but seeing happy satisfied faces in your day-to-day roles can be very rewarding. Much of my experience of working in government offices had been of people so bound up in official process that they appeared to spend a lot of time chasing their tails. There seemed to be fewer moments of triumph. I had often wondered what I was actually achieving in the big scheme of things. But the lure of better pay and more flexible working hours was enticing so I returned to work for the government in an environment that was extremely different to the buzz of the pharmacy.

The section I went to work in was heavily bound up in bureaucratic red tape. My new boss looked very important as he strode through the office in his immaculate uniform and shiny shoes. He was pleasant enough but was a stickler for rules and routines. I felt like a rat running around on a treadmill in a little cage. The job was not very demanding but strict security procedures had to be followed and precision was everything. Before long I became dreadfully bored, stifled by the tedium of the office rituals.

In search of some light relief I chummed up with the manager of another section whose office was near mine. He had a good sense of humour and seemed a great deal more relaxed than the guy I was working for. I confided in him that our chats were like a sanity break because so many of the people in the office seemed programmed to conform and perform within predictable boundaries. They were like robots coming into the office day after day, with little change to their routine. My manager friend laughed, and joked, *"You'd better be careful you don't become one of them."*

Creating space in your mind

A calm voice kept telling me to relax and breathe deeply. I felt a bit irritated, thinking, 'I don't have time to listen to this.' A friend had lent me a relaxation tape. She must have thought I needed it. I persevered because I figured that someone who doesn't have time to listen to a relaxation tape is probably the one who most needs it.

Adapting to life in a stepfamily had meant big changes in our home life. In addition to this, I was studying for my fourth grade AMEB saxophone examination. My brain was becoming a bit like the shop window, crowded with stuff.

Obeying the voice, I lay on the couch breathing deeply. The voice talked me through the relaxation of various body parts, and when it got to my toes, it assumed that I was now completely physically relaxed. Then the voice asked me to clear my mind. I figured that wouldn't be very hard at all, but no matter how hard I tried, I kept thinking. Little unimportant and trivial thoughts kept jumping into my head. I worried that I had truly become a society robot, so distracted by the busy world around me I couldn't empty my cluttered mind!

The irony of all this was that I was now living with a man who was relaxed and easy going yet incredibly creative. He encouraged me to find things that I was passionate about. He supported my musical endeavours and was not fussed by my inclination to frequent changes in employment. I admired his passion for music and liked that he was not seeking others' approval of what he was doing. He played and sang exactly the same whether or not he had an audience. He also had a tendency toward nonconformity that brought light relief after a day with the society robots.

He seemed to be able to relax at the drop of a hat. He would come home from a day of teaching, happy to do chores, play with the kids and then flop onto the couch and chill out at a moment's notice. When I told him I admired these qualities in him, he assured me that I had the same capability. I wondered if I was trying too hard.

Using both sides of my brain

"You've played this enough times now. You know it off by heart. You don't need the music." And with that Simon removed the music from the stand. I was playing one of my examination pieces for what seemed like the millionth time.

With my saxophone exam fast approaching, I had began to ramp-up my practice routine. The fourth grade pieces were challenging and I played them over and over. Before long everyone in the house had the tunes on their brain. I had my music stand set up in the lounge room and I played at every opportunity.

Simon was right. I played to the end of the piece without the music. "How did that feel?" he asked. "Wow! It felt pretty good," I said. In fact, the more I played, the better it felt.

Taking the music away was the best thing Simon could have done. He explained that by removing the visual distraction of the sheet music, he was encouraging me to engage the creative part of my brain. It was like another part of me came to life. I closed my eyes and heard myself play like never before. I was amazed that something so simple could be so powerful. It made me wonder what else my creative brain was capable of.

Space and stimulation

It took a while before all of these experiences came together in my mind to form a clearer picture. When I was relaxed and open-minded I was in a better position to access my intuition, which led me to meet a man who helped me to get in touch with the creative part of my mind. The right side of my brain was stimulated when the sheet music was removed from my line of sight. Before this, I had never thought of myself as being creative and it is amazing how this paved the way for my innovative thinking in property investment. While my experience with music may seem unrelated, it is surprising how much you can achieve when you begin to glimpse your own creative potential.

Decorating the shop window made me recognise the value in starting with a clean slate. Strangely, this exercise rekindled the imagination I had been blessed with as a child. I realised that our minds need space, a fresh platform on which to grow new ideas. My imagination couldn't flourish when my head was jammed full of thoughts. With practice, I was more easily able to relax, clear my head and allow ideas to flow and images to appear on the screen of my mind.

But as well as space our imagination also needs stimulation. It is the contrast and diversity of our surroundings that fuels our creative mind. Working in a fixed and routine environment had me feeling like a robot and stifled my creativity. While too much mental clutter can inhibit the imagination, a lack of variety can stifle our artistic spirit.

> *Our capacity to thrive is reliant on our willingness to continually search for enough diversity to stimulate thought, while also allowing ourselves space to become creative by regularly clearing the clutter of our everyday world from our minds.*

When the answer comes before the question

Sometimes we get answers or clues that we do not yet have a question for. We instinctively store information until we have a reason to use it. We sometimes forget how much we know and, at times, our **knowing** comes from sources that seem elusive. I have friends with extremely enquiring, analytical minds who like to understand the science behind things. They like to know where information comes from and have a hard time relying on something like a *gut feeling* or *intuition* because it may appear to have no credible source. Some may think of serendipity as a quirk of fate but, in my view, it happens naturally when we are open-minded, appreciative and excited by the adventure that life offers.

Whatever your situation right now, it is important to remember that you are not starting from scratch. Your life experiences all hold lessons. Without problems we would have no need to search for solutions; without questions we would not look for answers. Part of the fun of life is piecing together clues as we anticipate the next boom: a new job, a new mate or another achievement that holds meaning.

With the right attitude we can make anything we want out of our lives. During this time, I felt that everything that happened to me, no matter how seemingly trivial, was an opportunity for me to grow and learn. My life was very ordinary in many ways and yet I knew that my attitude towards life was spiralling upwards. Somehow I *knew* that this was going to make all the difference.

Pursuing diversity
Taking chances and chasing opportunity

Opportunity on a platter

Life provides a smorgasbord of choice. There are so many career paths, hobbies, sports and special interests, so many adventures and life experiences to choose from. The choice is endless. Opportunities cross our path every moment of every day; in fact, it is often not when we are searching madly but when we are feeling easy going and happy, that things are just about handed to us on a platter.

My childhood dreams of singing like my idol Mary Poppins were rekindled when it dawned on me that I was now married to an experienced and talented musician. In his spare time, Simon loves to sit and strum his guitar and sing. When he found out I also liked singing, he encouraged me to join him. He helped me establish my vocal range and taught me to sing harmony. He invited me to practice with one of the bands he was involved with and I jumped at the chance. Although I was playing alto saxophone in a concert band at the time, I was new to performing as a singer (unless you count singing in front of the living room mirror into a hairbrush). Rehearsing was fun, so once I had enough songs in my repertoire, I agreed to perform with my normal enthusiasm coupled with blissful ignorance.

The show must go on

The butterflies in my stomach were getting larger and more boisterous by the second. I was feeling nauseous and my palms were sweating. Standing backstage waiting for our band to go on stage and perform to an audience of a couple of hundred people saw my nervousness reach a new peak. Playing sax or providing backing vocals was one thing, but the thought of singing the lead to such a large audience was suddenly terrifying.

Simon had played in bands since he was a teenager and the rest of the boys in the band were also experienced musicians and used to performing. I was a mere novice and was beginning to question my sanity. Why on earth had I thought this was a good idea? It was all very well practicing in someone's garage, but now there was a very real live audience waiting to be entertained.

Feeling frozen with fear was not something I had expected. I had to think fast how to overcome it. I figured I had two options — fight or flight. Flight was appealing. I could run and hide in the ladies' room. But then I remembered Simon had designed the set lists for the evening to give me plenty of opportunity to sing the lead. This was what I had wanted: an opportunity to be a singer, and yet I felt petrified. The band had all put effort into practice, preparation and planning for the event. I couldn't run. I had to stay and fight my fear.

Simon could see I was giving myself a hard time. He suggested I focus on the first line of my first song. He told me to just repeat it over and over in my head. The rest will just flow on, he said. I took his advice and started to go over and over my first line. The remaining minutes before we went on seemed to take forever, but at least I had made my decision. The show must go on.

Finally we were directed to take our place under the bright lights on the stage. I didn't know whether to feel relief that the waiting was over or scared of the still-rising feeling of fear. But it was too late to run.

Simon had planned to sing the lead in the first song. This turned out to be a good move as I stood like a statue on the stage trying to order my body to look relaxed and natural. The crowd applauded enthusiastically after the opening number. Then Simon strummed the opening chords of my first song. This was my big moment. I sang the first line and my voice sounded croaky and foreign. Not like the lovely smooth voice I had produced in practice sessions. But Simon's advice paid off. I kept going and my voice got stronger.

The night ended up going really well. With each new song I gained more confidence. The audience danced and applauded. They were having a good time. My fear gradually melted away and I really got into it. People in the audience stood and called out for more. This was fun. What had I been so afraid of?

No regrets

Once I got my nerves under control I really started to love performing. I wondered if this could be my new career but with several more gigs under my belt, the novelty began to wear off when I realised the time commitment involved.

The regular practice sessions were a lot of fun but doing a gig took significant dedication. We'd set up a few hours before the gig, usually late afternoon around 4 or 5pm. Once the last number for the evening was over, normally around midnight or 1am, it still took least an hour or more to pack up all the sound equipment and instruments and load them into the vehicles. Then the band members would sometimes go for a cuppa or a hot dog just to unwind, which meant it was quite common to get home around 3am or later.

Much as I enjoyed the experience of playing in the band, I questioned whether I wanted to spend so much time working at night. My children were still young at the time and weekends were precious. I didn't want to spend them sleeping half of the day. But

I'm so glad I grabbed the opportunity to experience a glimpse of life 'on the stage'.

The glamorous images I had held of performing at night as a singer had lost a little of their shine, but I was happy because it was another thing I could tick off my list. I didn't want to reach a point in my life where I regretted not having tried things.

Can't walk and chew gum

Some people think that you have to be brilliant at something before you try it, yet a trait I find a lot of successful people have in common is their willingness to have a go at something without feeling a need to perfect it. Simon understood this when he invited me into the band. He and I both knew that I was not exactly Madonna, but I had enough of what it takes to entertain a crowd. I could sing and look interesting enough as I moved in time with the music.

One thing many people probably didn't notice was that I was pretty useless at playing percussion and singing at the same time. I could bang the tambourine in time with the music, and I could sing in tune, but do you think I could do both at once and stay with the beat? I never did master it. I joked that I couldn't walk and chew gum at the same time. But Simon and I believe in smoke and mirrors. If it looks good enough to make a favourable impression, why beat yourself up trying to get it all perfect? I think if I strived for perfection in everything, I wouldn't try many things at all. Being up on stage would have remained an unfulfilled dream.

Now I'd temporarily ruled out becoming a famous singer, I looked around for the next opportunity and found it in the newspaper.

Lucky Laura

Her dress clung seductively to her body and shimmered as she walked under the bright lights of the hotel foyer. I nudged Simon to take a look but then realised he had already noticed her. Heads turned as she moved towards the reception desk.

It was below freezing outside and, like many local women, my winter evening attire consisted of several unexciting layers, including a black coat, black trousers and sensible shoes. This lady looked stunning, as though she was about to attend the Academy Awards. She was an extraordinary spectacle in my ordinary world.

Ready to job-hop yet again, I had responded to an advertisement for sales representatives and was at the hotel to attend a product launch. Simon had come along to help me check it out. As I enquired at the reception desk, Laura turned to greet me. Her smile was as enchanting as her outfit, and it turned out that she was the main speaker of the event I was attending. She introduced herself and invited us to join her in the function room.

Laura's presentation was dynamic and her style engaging. The products she was promoting held great appeal for me, but I think she could have been selling fluff and I would still have wanted to work with and learn from her. I had a hunch that this woman had a lot to offer.

Born lucky

My hunch paid off as I discovered that Laura's magnetism went far beyond the way she looked. After I had worked with her for several months, it was evident she was a high achiever. She won awards, set sales records, and developed strong and productive associations with work colleagues. She always managed to look great and had a knack for making an entrance with her engaging smile and beguiling charm.

I had met people like Laura before and I was intrigued to find out what made them tick. Were some people born with the odds stacked in their favour? Were some babies just destined to become charismatic, confident, clever and capable adults? Up until now I had assumed that people like Laura were just born lucky.

One weekend, when she hosted a function at her home, I asked her how she managed to get so many things right in her life. "How do you do it? You juggle all the pressures in your life and come up with great results. Were you just born lucky?" I complained I was busy with work and trying to balance my family and social life. I wished I had more hours in the day. Laura's response was simple: "We all have 24 hours in a day and it takes just as much time to be unlucky as it does to be lucky."

As was so often the case, her popularity got in the way. Someone broke into our conversation and I was left intrigued, yet frustrated, not completely understanding what she meant. Her husband was standing with us and sensed my frustration. He knew I admired Laura. He confided in me that she had not always been so lucky. Her childhood and teenage years had not been a bed of roses. Life had dished up some challenging experiences for Laura and yet now, in her mid-thirties, she was on fire: happy, prosperous and successful.

Permission to thrive

Laura's real forte was dealing with people. She oozed confidence and charisma. I was fascinated by her ability to capture the attention of those around her and bring them around to her point of view. I asked her to coach me and she agreed. Something we did together that worked really well was role play. She would pretend to be a customer and I would practice my sales spiels on her. She would then challenge me with every objection she could think of. Then we would swap. I would pretend to be the customer and she would feed me spiels that she had used effectively with her own customers. She taught me to put myself in the customer's shoes and consider how I liked to be treated.

She also trained me to train others and present to groups, and coached me on reframing and dealing with difficult people. She encouraged me to actively listen to people so that I could accurately give them feedback on my understanding of what they wanted. This was especially relevant when I began to train and coach others. She reminded me of the importance in finding something I liked about a person so that I was always ready with a sincere compliment. She reminded me that people are much more open to learning from someone they like, someone who has taken a genuine interest in them.

Laura demonstrated an immense personal power because of her ability to bring out the best in others around her. She explained to me that in order to inspire others to shine, you must first give yourself permission to thrive. This concept seemed somewhat counter to the humility and selflessness I had been encouraged to embrace in religion classes at school. Saints had been portrayed as selfless and humble, and had often suffered some horrible fate. As a child I had found some of the stories far from inspiring. Now I knew why.

Of all the lessons Laura taught me, this was the most important. She told me that in order to ignite passion, and recognise strength and potential in others, you must first feel and see these things in yourself.

The value in pursuing diversity

Another thing I loved about Laura was that she had an innovative approach to her work and business. She was always developing new models. She regularly found new ways to present a concept at training or a new slant on an existing product or service. She understood the benefits of habit and repetition, in that they can save time and energy and make a model appear more replicable to others, but she continued to explore opportunities to improve her training models along with her presentation style.

She understood that models, habits and patterns present both risk and opportunity. In sameness (repetition) we find comfort and ease but, over time, we can become complacent and, in the absence of the stimulation that variety provides, we lose our creativity. When we repeat a sequence successfully several times over, it is easy to assume that this will continue to work on an ongoing basis. But habits, models or patterns can cause one to become so robotic that the process does not arouse innovative thinking. Even the very best models, habits and patterns eventually become obsolete simply because human beings are programmed to invent and create. We can't expect to find the next best thing and expect it to be the best forever. We are wonderfully innovative creatures and our imagination holds the key to our personal growth and zest for life.

Laura encouraged me to embrace a more dynamic approach to life. She prompted me to observe the difference between people who are creatures of habit and more set in their ways, to those who shift and change what they do, where they go and whom they mix with. She used examples of people who live long-term in the same house or work in the same job for the same firm for an extensive period of time. She compared this with someone who had a broader experience and had pursued diversity in their work or home surroundings, moved around more, travelled extensively, mixed with other dynamic people and honed their interpersonal and social skills. It was easy to see who exposed themself to greater opportunity.

Shifters and changers are much more adaptable and groundbreaking in their thinking, and rather than being afraid of change they embrace the opportunities that it presents. Laura was a shifter and changer. She had studied psychology and worked in this field in varying roles before moving to a sales environment. She moved from another city and lived close to Sydney's CBD because of the variety of interesting people she met there.

The many lessons I learned from Laura are still fresh in my mind today. She encouraged me to spread my wings. I have since met other people like her who have inspired me to seek opportunity in all that I do, and I have included more stories in chapter 15, *Magnificent mentors*.

The spice of my life

My propensity for job-hopping and trying lots of different things may not make sense to those who crave a predictable existence but it has provided constant opportunities for me to have fresh experiences and improve the way I live my life. I was getting a look in the door at many different work environments, and had the added benefit of meeting lots of intrinsically interesting people—more *lucky links*.

I sometimes wished that I would one day wake up knowing what I wanted to do for the rest of my life but now I understand the benefit of exploring a wide variety of jobs, hobbies and adventures. I'm so glad that I continued to flit around from one activity to another because it has helped me to be more definite about what I want from life and clearer about what makes me happy. I have pursued many opportunities that have allowed me to refine my preferences and I no longer crave an answer to what I might want to do when I grow up. I hope I never take life so seriously that I want to settle on one answer. Variety is absolutely the spice of my life.

Pursuing diversity presents a stimulating mix of risk and opportunity. Something that may be perceived as risky by one person can appear as an opportunity to another. Through experience, I found it best not to base a decision merely on the opinions and experiences of others. For example, years before I worked with Laura, I had often considered that working in sales and earning commission would be fun, but well-meaning friends had dissuaded me because their perception was that working for commission was risky. Sometimes it is hard to recognise risk from opportunity until you give it a try. I didn't earn a lot of money working in direct sales with Laura but I had a lot of fun and learned so much that it gave me the confidence to embark on a whole new learning curve—one that was to cause an enormous positive shift in the way I thought about money.

Embracing new possibilities

Allowing your mind to be open to new expectations

There is so much more inside our minds than we suspect. There is so much more outside than we are capable of being curious about.

From *Using your Brain for a Change* by Richard Bandler

A belief challenged

"It will take me years to read all this stuff," I complained. I was working in educational book sales, which brought me into an environment where I was surrounded by avid readers and beautiful books. Most of my colleagues had a great deal more formal education than I did. Many were university-educated and I envied their ability to quickly soak up vast quantities of information. Although I adored reading, I felt like an imposter as I read at a snail's pace and struggled to find enough time to read.

Many of the top salespeople attributed much of their success to reading inspirational and motivational books, so my recommended reading list was steadily growing. I felt that my academic capacity was overwhelmingly ordinary, restricted by my inferior reading ability.

A girl on my sales team told me that she had recently done a speed-reading course. She became very animated as she talked about *the potential of the human mind. She was told on the course that our brains can take in a great deal more information in a much shorter time than most people realise. She explained some of the techniques and expounded the benefits they offered in improved reading ability in terms of both speed and retention.*

It struck me how different her attitude towards reading was to mine. Her belief was that reading quickly was easy. Mine was that reading took a lot of time. She had enormous confidence, and I had low expectations.

My belief that I was a slow reader was a major impediment in itself. Because I had, for years, been reinforcing that I was a slow reader, I was setting myself up for reading at a snail's pace for the rest of my life. Not only was I telling friends about it, I realised I was constantly reinforcing it in my head whenever the subject arose. *"I'm a slow reader, I take ages to read anything."*

When my friend spoke of the enormous potential of our minds, it reminded me that many of the beliefs that get implanted in our subconscious are not necessarily based on fact and not all are useful. I recalled the benefits I had received years earlier when I used affirmations and practised mental rehearsal. It was time for me to review what I was thinking about and programming into my subconscious.

Great expectations

You may think that the next logical step would have been for me to enrol myself in a speed-reading course, but no, I decided instead to put my mind to the test. Using affirmations and a change of attitude, I set about seeing how far I could shift my reality and improve the quantity and quality of my reading *without* attending any courses.

Remembering Laura's words, I decided to better utilise each 24 hours by maximising my reading time. I began reading at night, instead of watching television.

To add strength to my new expectation, I adopted simple affirmations like *I am a fast, efficient reader*. I repeated this both in my head and in writing. I also focused on the benefits that would come from being able to read more quickly. I visualised my 'pile of books to be read' growing smaller as I read them and put them back on the bookshelf. I saw myself smiling, feeling proud of my new ability to read with as much speed and enjoyment as I wished.

My experiment paid off! Within a couple of months I had finished half the books on my list, where previously this would have taken me a year. With practice, I improved the pace of my reading and my ability to digest a lot of information in a shorter time. My improved reading capacity encouraged me to become more mindful of self-limiting beliefs. It was becoming clearer that I had not been behind the door when the brains were passed out. I just hadn't been using all of mine.

Reading about neuro-linguistic programming, including material by Richard Bandler, provided further reinforcement that I had a great deal more control over my thought processes than I had previously believed. If I hadn't been making the most of my brain, now was a good time to change that.

Great expectations were building within me. If this worked for improving my reading, what other areas of my life could I improve?

Beliefs versus expectations

Our beliefs and expectations are fed by many sources. Sometimes our beliefs are not actual truths but thoughts we have adopted through habit and repetition. Have you ever adopted a belief as being *the truth*, only to find at some point in the future that it was an illusion; a thought process you embraced and repeated until it became your reality until something or someone came along and challenged it?

Beliefs can hold us back when we cling to them for too long. They can cause us to resist change when fresh ideas or opportunities are presented to us. Although the concept of speed reading was not new to me, it came to my attention when I was open to change. Our beliefs are often challenged when we develop a greater need or a new desire.

We form our perceptions and beliefs from the knowledge we have available to us. I didn't believe that speed reading was something I was capable of until my friend came along and challenged my belief. My potential for growth and self-improvement increased as I exposed myself to new ideas.

As kids and teenagers our ignorance of many of 'the facts of life' can be blissful because it allows us to have more positive expectations. **Ignorance can be blissful when there is an absence of self-limiting beliefs.** That's why kids generally are more cheerful than adults. They don't take life so seriously. Adults are expected to know more. We cram so-called 'facts' into our head and turn them into 'beliefs'.

Beliefs are often based on our current perception of reality and on what is considered 'realistic'. We are often encouraged not to bite off more than we can chew and some will suggest that it is best not to expect too much so as to avoid disappointment. But our world is constantly changing and expanding because people embrace positive expectations and open their minds up to new possibilities. Imagination, together with positive expectations and new perceptions of what is possible, is where invention and innovation come from. Many things we take for granted today, like electricity, plane travel, mobile phones, computers and the internet, would not be around if people had not shifted their belief of what was probable into a positive expectation of what was possible.

My most significant achievements as an adult have been born of dreams and ideas that, to some, may have appeared unrealistic. For example, when I dreamt about singing and performing on stage, some may have thought that would be unrealistic for someone with little formal singing training. And if I had chosen to be influenced by the limiting beliefs of others, rather than developing my own expectations, I would never have given it a go. Instead, I chose to pay attention to people who encouraged me to chase my dreams, and the experience built my confidence which paved the way for bolder imaginings.

Possibilities vs probabilities

It is easy to develop a tendency to base our expectations on past experiences or on the recounted experiences of others. We are often encouraged by others to be realistic. But rather than getting caught up in other people's views of what is realistic, doesn't it make more sense to decide what you want and embrace new possibilities on the subject? While many would suggest that we should base our expectations on probabilities rather than possibilities, those who achieve the extraordinary form their expectations based on what is possible, regardless of the expectations of others.

There is a big difference between expecting what is probable and imagining what is possible. Looking at what is probable requires an assessment of what is feasible or plausible based on statistics or the measured performance or results of a prior situation or event. Looking at what is possible leans toward potential and promise. It is a more futuristic approach rather than historical, with ideas emanating from the imagination rather than an assessment of facts. Probabilities require you to look back in time; possibilities require you to look forward.

Don't let other people's version of reality cramp your style. Embrace new possibilities and create your own.

What do you imagine you are capable of?

The human mind is capable of powerful focus. When we focus on something for long enough and with enough intensity we can blow things up out of proportion. This works both in the positive and the negative. You can see yourself getting sicker or imagine yourself becoming well; picture yourself going backwards financially or imagine yourself prospering.

It is often an awareness of what we don't want that leads us to know more clearly what we *do* want, but that is where the negative attention should cease. The law of attraction makes perfect sense. It is worth being mindful of what we give our attention to. When we focus on perceived weaknesses or things we don't want we add power to them. When we focus on what is wanted with positive expectation we can embrace new possibilities.

With each new milestone in human achievement we are reminded that we are capable of much more than we sometimes give ourselves credit for. Our greatest achievements often follow our greatest challenges.

> *What we achieve can often spring from the questions we ask ourselves. Instead of asking yourself, What do I **believe** I am capable of? Ask yourself, What do I **imagine** I am capable of?*

The launching pad
Designing your own destiny before someone else does it for you

Wake-up call

"You're brainwashed. I can see it in your eyes." Her words struck me like a slap in the face. Now onto my third network marketing company, I was spruiking the benefits of joining 'the business' to a customer. My pitch generally created interest or a polite rebuff, so her response startled me.

Anger rose up within me. I felt this woman was labelling me as someone who couldn't think for herself. But then she told me about her own involvement in a network marketing company. She had done well and made money. She had attended meetings where everyone clapped and cheered, and this had made her feel good. She'd been told she had what it takes to be successful. But one day it had dawned on her how brainwashed she had become. Constantly prospecting, she used to approach just about every person she met as a potential customer or consultant. The business had become all-consuming, dominating her *social life and at the end of the day the company called the shots. They controlled what and how she sold and without the company and its products, her business could not exist. The idea that she was running her own business was, in many respects, just an illusion.*

As she told her story I realised, that it was also my story. I recalled some of the conferences I had attended. I too had clapped and cheered and sung along with the hype songs. It had almost felt like being in church. A string of certificates on my office wall had made me feel important. I had done well but was not making the sort of money that had been flaunted by those who had already *made it*.

This encounter was like a wake-up call. She was right! The idea that I was running my own business was an illusion. I had no control over the products and had to abide by company rules. I felt the pressure to conform was stifling my creative spirit.

It seems strange that when enough people tell you something, you think it must be the truth. I thought I had found *the answer*, but I was still dancing to someone else's tune. I had unwittingly become a society robot once again. I'd been programmed to copy those above me and entice newcomers to follow in my footsteps.

Every stick has two ends, however, and on the other end of this one I considered that network marketing hadn't been all bad. I'd had some flexibility in my hours and was able to do some of my work from home. I had enjoyed the interaction with people and the learning curves. My improved reading skills had come as a result of the *lucky links* I'd made associating with other motivated salespeople. My confidence had grown when it came to dealing with people. I was less shy and more prepared to initiate conversation. I had learned a great deal and made many new friends.

But on the rough end of the stick I didn't want to feel brainwashed and constantly coaxed into conformity so I took time to consider what the opposite of that was. I wanted to think for myself and design my own destiny instead of feeling that someone else was making decisions for me.

Slotting into the tiniest *sliver of pie* was still my dream. I wanted to join that very small percentage of the population who are prepared to call their own shots, make a lot of money and enjoy a lifestyle that is laced with fun and freedom. Trying to achieve something so rare by competing with thousands of others didn't make any sense.

Calling the shots

The character of Mary Poppins appealed to me when I was a child because she was prepared to speak her mind and express herself in unique ways. She made decisions and wasn't looking around at others for direction.

When I've been passive, led by others and let someone else call the shots I haven't needed to take much responsibility. But I became frustrated when I felt I was giving others what they wanted and not getting what I wanted.

The motivational and inspirational books I had read contained a common thread: the idea that those who achieve extraordinary success do so by travelling their own road and designing their own destiny. I didn't know how I was going to do it but I was finding more clues at every turn.

A powerful launching pad

The next story is of one of my shorter stints with an employer. I worked with a guy called Barry for less than two weeks. It is not that I was commitment phobic but more that I knew paid work is easy to come by when you display mild levels of intelligence and are open-minded and personable. I didn't see the point of staying in a job that I didn't like or working with people that I didn't get along with.

Some of the people who have read this brief account of my encounter with Barry have wanted more information about him. But it is not appropriate or important that you know more about Barry or any of the other characters featured in this book. What is important is what I learned from the experience.

Some of our most memorable *cranky attacks* provide the most powerful launching pads.

Bossy Barry

Barry glared at me as he stood over my desk. He cast his eyes up and down my frame, conveying a message that said, You'll never amount to anything, *and then he spoke.* "You'll spend the rest of your working years in a boring government job on a basic income." *His words hammered the message home.*

Barry's reaction to my imminent departure had me gobsmacked. He was angry because I had just told him I was quitting and returning to work in the public service. Barry's managerial style was to rule with an iron fist, so high staff turnover was a problem. Two other members of staff were also leaving, but I think I copped the brunt of Barry's frustration because I had only lasted a week and a half. It was obvious that we were experiencing a personality clash, and I was kicking myself for not following my gut feeling and leaving after the first day.

Music to calm the angry beast

When I got home Barry's words hit me and I felt my fury rising. I was livid. Who did Barry think he was to sum up my future like that? Barry was such an angry beast. He made *me* feel angry!

I paced around the house for a while blowing off steam but after a while I began to feel despondent, wondering, *Will I ever make it? Was I just chasing my tail, spinning around from one job to the next?* But rather than harbour feelings of hopelessness, I lightened my load by discussing it with Simon. Regurgitating the experience made me mad again. "*How dare he talk to me like that,*" I complained. Strangely, being angry felt better than feeling hopeless.

Simon, in his wisdom, could see the power in my anger and suggested that I turn it to good use. "*He's added fuel to your fire. Why don't you utilise your energy to prove him wrong?*"

I knew Simon was right. I could feel the emotion surging within me. I wanted to find relief from my frustration of not knowing what to do next. I thought of all the strategies I normally employed to lift my spirits, like engaging in some heavy exercise, talking with friends or mellowing into a glass of wine.

But none of those things appealed, so I finally settled for some music. The piece I selected was one I had recently performed with the concert band I played in. It always made me feel so good and I wasn't quite sure why. I could listen to it over and over again.

For some reason, it feels good to play music really loudly when you're cranky, so I set the volume high and let the sound reverberate throughout the living room. The beat was slow and rhythmic and the harmonic sequence repetitive. The melody seemed to ebb and flow. It would build up, then ease off. It was not until the end of the piece that it reached the high notes that brought a sense of victory.

The music, *Pachelbel's Canon*, was hypnotic, and a surprising feeling of relief washed over me. Its triumphant sounds strengthened my resolve. I **knew** I was going to prove Barry wrong.

Ego is not a dirty word

Securing a contract in a government office seemed like heaven following my experience with Bossy Barry. My new colleagues were friendly and I found being back in a more stable, routine office environment had its advantages. It felt good to know exactly how much and how often I would get paid. Little did I know at the time that this job was to hold such significance. It was to be my longest ever temp assignment (over two years) and my last stint working for a wage.

Ironically, my work was not always stimulating and some days were mind-numbingly dull, so when an opportunity came up to attend a two-day staff development program, I jumped at it. Anything to get away from the clock-watching, tea-drinking tedium I had become accustomed to.

"This isn't me," I thought. I was in denial. I had just completed my first personality profile test. We were told to complete the form as quickly

as possible, not to ponder anything too much. Just give a quick gut reaction. Once we were finished we had to plot our answers onto a graph that would rank us into our strongest of four main categories, then a more specific individual profile. My results were completely surprising to me. I thought I'd either made a mistake or the test didn't work for everyone.

There were about 120 people and we were divided into four groups according to the strongest traits apparent from the test. The test was designed to help us understand ourselves better and get a clearer picture of our strengths and weaknesses. As I sat and laughed with the other people in my group I realised I was sitting at a table of my favourite people in the office. I was indeed in the right group. This was where I belonged. The test was spot-on.

The things I learned from this experience were like a breath of fresh air. The results of my test suggested that I thrive on variety and enjoy a shifting and changing work environment. I couldn't believe how apt this was. No wonder my mind was going numb in the stable and routine environment of the public service. My penchant for jumping from one workplace or occupation to the next finally made perfect sense. Variety keeps me energised. Without it I risked becoming uninteresting and stale, just like my job.

As part of the program, we also engaged in exercises that were designed to help us develop a better understanding of the strengths and weaknesses of other personality types so we could discover what motivates them and see how their priorities were likely to differ from our own. I noticed how well I related to people who were similar in personality to me. The people in my group were, in my view, the most interesting and dynamic people in the office.

The personality profile had the effect of boosting my self-esteem. Sitting in a boring job hadn't helped in that area so I was ripe for a lift. Identifying my strengths made me feel pretty good about myself. Instead of stagnating at my desk I decided to let more of my personality shine out for others to see.

In the past when I observed others who seemed to have a natural ability to do things that I couldn't do, I used to think that my job, as a human, was to strive to be good at everything. It was a great relief when I realised I get much better results when I lean on my strengths and work with others who have different abilities and fortes to mine.

Many people had told me that having an ego is a bad thing. But the word ego relates to our personality and character traits and our sense of self. Ego is not in itself bad. Someone who displays a great deal of self-interest may be described as having big ego but my ego was becoming more precious every day. I never again wanted it to slip onto the floor under my desk. I wanted to nurture it by getting more in touch with my skills and strengths and enjoying the personality I was born with so I could let the real me emerge.

When my ego was flat I was of less value to others. With my ego in better shape I was much more interesting and fun to be around.

Every stick has two ends

Everyone has their own agenda and our chances of success are greatly enhanced as we increase our ability to harmonise with others. When I understood more about my own skills and more clearly identified my preferences it made this process much easier. I could link up with others who liked what I had to offer and vice versa. When I pay attention to my gut feelings it is easier to match up with people who are on the same wavelength as me and who have an agenda that complements mine.

It's hard to form a clear picture of *who you are* when you are not really sure what you're good at. Just as it is hard to design your own destiny when you don't know exactly what you want. I had a big picture of what I wanted and each one of these experiences was providing me with valuable clues.

The variety of my life was enabling me to view the world from various vantage points. Even though I continued to stumble onto things that I disliked, I invariably discovered aspects within those experiences that I enjoyed and wanted more of. Just as every stick has two ends, every subject or experience has positive and negative aspects. Without that contrast we would not have access to such a wide range of choices.

Each new job gave me a chance to further refine my preferences and priorities. I was able to look at the rough end of the stick—the things I didn't like—and then look for solutions or advantages. For example, one of the good things about having a boring job meant that I craved mental stimulation. I spent my lunch hours in the library and read as many books as I could on the subjects of money and real-estate investment.

Knowing that I didn't want to feel controlled or brainwashed made me realise how empowering it is to make more decisions. Even small decisions shifted me to a new vantage point. Exercising my freedom of choice to a larger extent made me feel more in control.

When we come across people like Bossy Barry it is so tempting to want to blame them for turning us into fuming angry beasts. Barry's words hit a raw nerve yet they had a wonderfully powerful effect. My anger fuelled my desire to improve my financial status far and beyond Barry's predictions. The next time someone says or does something that makes you feel angry, see it as an opportunity to more clearly define what you DO want.

My increased self-awareness and improved understanding of others enhanced my self-confidence. With this I felt more inclined to make more decisions, which in turn provided yet more variety and choice and enhanced my feeling of freedom.

Design your destiny

If you are serious about pursuing freedom, try this exercise. Draw up a two-column table. On the left side, *The Cranky column*, make a list of things that irritate you or make you feel angry; then on the right side, *The Freedom column*, write down positive attitudes or actions that enhance your feelings of freedom, thereby countering your negative thoughts.

What you write in the *Freedom column* has to be something you can see yourself achieving. For example, if you don't like war you may be tempted to write 'World peace' in your *Freedom column*. But the idea is to write things that will enhance your freedom of choice so don't write things that you cannot personally imagine yourself doing or achieving. Keep it simple, especially in the beginning.

Here is an example and it is important that you understand that it is not designed to be directive, but more to stimulate thought. Write things in your *Freedom column* that will make you feel empowered to effect positive changes. And remember that small changes are better than no change. Some people seem so focused on effecting huge change that they are too impatient to move slowly at first. If you want to move mountains, start practicing on molehills.

The Launching Pad exercise

Cranky column	Freedom column
Don't like feeling controlled or brainwashed and being told what to do	Make more decisions, both little and big. More decisions lead to more choices leading us to feel greater freedom
Don't like people who take themselves too seriously	Lighten up and look on the bright side of life. Seek to mix with people who have a sense of humour
Don't want to be lonely	Go out and get a life. Make sure you greet at least seven people a day and smile more often
Didn't like being bored	Seek brain food and mental stimulation eg, reading and mixing with interesting people

Feel stifled by conformity	You are free to think for yourself and even if you perceive that your choice of action is limited, remember your choice of thought is vast
I'm feeling sorry for myself	Remind yourself that you are free: free to choose what you focus upon; free to shift the direction of your thoughts; free to look for things that you like; and free to look for reasons to feel good
Don't like war	Pursue harmonious relationships. Find peace within and allow others to live life on their terms

The *Cranky column* looks like a big whinge fest, yet when I read the *Freedom column* it stirs feelings of release and liberation. The reason for this exercise is because we sometimes fail to see the obvious. Anger doesn't stop wars. Fighting against something only creates more angst. The only way to resolve issues in your *Cranky column* is to look at the opposite; in other words take your focus from the rough end of the stick and pick up the right end.

The 90/10 rule

In his book *Awaken the Giant Within* Anthony Robbins talks of spending no more than 10 per cent of your time on a problem and at least 90 per cent of your time on the solution. This reinforces the idea of *The Launching Pad*. The *Cranky column* should take no more than 10 per cent of your focus. When you get good at this it will take an even smaller percentage. When you are putting 90 per cent, or more, of your time, energy and focus into finding solutions and pursuing advantages, you will truly understand why I have labelled this exercise **The Launching Pad**. It is a powerful way of living and one that can create a significant turning point in your life, as it did for me.

Destiny by design

Destiny by design means directing your life with clear intentions so you feel you are in control of circumstances rather than the other way around. Designing your own destiny means having priorities and **clarity** about what is wanted from each and every aspect of your life. When you manage this, it will free you up to notice more opportunities and that is where we are heading next.

The stories in the following chapter were interwoven time-wise with those in this chapter but I am presenting them in this order so that the concepts flow in a logical sequence. There was a huge momentum building during the first years of my second marriage. When I spent more time looking at solutions and advantages, a marvellous thing happened. I began to discover hidden potential and notice opportunities that I had been walking past every day. They were the type of opportunities that surround us all.

Hidden potential

Extending your awareness of the potential of the people and places that surround you

Unpolished gems

Have you ever been too busy to notice what's going on right under your nose? Early in my second marriage telltale signs had begun to appear. My house kept changing. The changes were subtle at first but became more dramatic as time went on. Within a year I was convinced. I had married a serial renovator!

In our first year of marriage we lived in three houses. The first house was mine. When Simon moved in, pictures appeared on the walls and strategically placed ornaments and pot plants adorned the living areas. Things that had been broken were fixed. The lawn was mown more regularly and the garden came to life. Within a few months the master bedroom sprouted a bay window.

The second house was Simon's. The kitchen was small and a bit poky but it too changed. Part of one of its walls disappeared, opening it up to the adjoining dining room—a definite improvement.

The third house was special. When we first walked through the front door, the agent congratulated us. He said that most people didn't get that far. The garden was overgrown and strewn with rubbish. A railing had fallen off the deck above the carport and lay across the driveway. As we made our way through the house, the rank atmosphere choked our airways. We parted cobwebs with our hands and stepped over little piles of droppings. The house had been empty for months and little creatures had made their home there. Curtains hung in rags from the windows and the bathrooms were filthy. The house was structurally sound and the price was right. It was dirt cheap!

We bought this house to better cater for our new family formation. Unlike the Brady Bunch, our six offspring didn't all live with us full-time but their comings and goings meant we needed room to move.

This was our first house purchase together and we saw it as an unpolished gem, full of hidden potential. The fact that it was all we could afford at the time was also a determining factor. Both our houses had fallen in value and were worth less than we'd paid for them. I was far from financially savvy at the time but both of us had at least the sense to avoid selling something at a loss. The rental returns then were good so this was a more appealing option. We became landlords by default.

The changes Simon made to our third home were significant. I came home from work one day to find one of the living room walls had disappeared completely. Within a couple of weeks, the toilet moved across the ensuite and there were new tiles on the walls as well as new fixtures and fittings. Not long after this the living room walls turned bright "envelope" yellow and the kitchen was painted an unusual shade of green.

Like our third home, my husband was an unpolished gem, full of surprises and hidden potential.

Now if you're thinking that you're at a disadvantage because you don't have a partner or perhaps you have one that you don't like very much, think again. Lucky links are all around us and every one of them has hidden potential. Sometimes they are right under our nose and we are too busy or too self-absorbed to notice their brilliance.

When we make the most of opportunities to reinvent ourselves and *renovate* certain aspects of our life, we keep moving, stay interesting and are more likely to attract other interesting and dynamic people into our life, people who are full of hidden potential.

Is it black or is it white?

A friend complained to me recently of his confusion in regard to the contradictions that often appear in a book of this type. I knew exactly what he meant. How can an author claim in one chapter that ignorance can be blissful and then go on to expound the value of self-awareness and education, through prolific reading, in another? When you take a step back and look at a bigger picture you can see that either can be true. Knowledge is valuable but sometimes too much of it can scare us. Sometimes we are better off not knowing too much if it means we are less afraid.

Life is full of contradictions, inconsistencies and opposites. When Simon and I bought our second house together we didn't know a lot about real estate. We had heard so many differing views. Expressions like *'Safe as houses'* or *'Put your money into bricks and mortar'* were comforting. Real estate was considered by many as a *safe* place to put your money. But if you listened to the naysayers there were plenty of stories of people who had *'lost their home'* or *'lost everything'* because they had overcommitted financially or bought 'a dud' property. Some will paint a black picture and others will paint a white bright one. The reality is that both are possible. You can make a lot of money or lose a lot of money investing in real estate. You can make or lose money doing lots of things.

Stark contrasts in life sometimes make choices appear either black or white yet the real opportunities are often hidden in the variety that lies in between. Sometimes we get confused when we observe so many shades of grey. We become overwhelmed by the diversity and choices available to us. When we want so much to make the *right* choice, we can become immobilised by a fear of making the *wrong* choice.

The thing that holds people back from making money is a fear of losing it. Something that carried me through the early stages of our real estate investing was my willingness to make decisions, whether or not they were *right*. The choices we made early on may not have been perfect but they provided learning curves that you can't get *just* from reading books. In our ignorance, Simon and I forged ahead with a little knowledge and a lot of passion and bravado. Our minds were open to sourcing the hidden potential around us.

Recognising opportunity and asking the right questions

The realisation that I was married to a man who was gifted at adding value to residential real estate wasn't a sudden *aha* moment, it was more a creeping awareness. The benefit of understanding and appreciating more about my own personality traits was kicking in more and my confidence was growing. I found myself noticing more of the strengths in the world around me.

A brightly coloured sign caught my eye. I was walking my dog and the sign was pointing up a little cul-de-sac that I walked past every day but had never paid much attention to. The sign read "Open for inspection". My curiosity led me up the little street to where a "For sale" sign was half hidden behind some rose bushes. The house looked stylish but scruffy. I decided it warranted further investigation.

The house was way out of our price range but I couldn't help but admire it. It had a contemporary feel with sunken living areas and cathedral ceilings. It had a delightful in-ground swimming pool concealed behind a brick wall in the back garden. The main bathroom was lined with cedar and smelled a bit like a sauna.

Back on the street out the front of the house I gazed at it longingly. The garden was unkempt and ivy had grown up onto the roof and dislodged part of the front fascia. The house had that unloved look that some rentals get after a few years. It was another unpolished gem — full of potential.

The house sat on the market for months. The price dropped significantly. People came in droves to look at it but it still didn't sell. It needed a lot of work. Simon looked at it and also saw its potential but it was still out of our reach financially—or so we thought.

My Dad came from Sydney to stay for a few days. He came to look at the house with us and could see why I'd fallen in love with it. Although the house had outdated decor, ugly wallpaper and threadbare carpet, Dad knew what Simon was capable of.

Dad suggested that I put in a low offer. I baulked at this, afraid it would insult the vendor or get the agent offside. Then Dad gave me my first lesson in negotiating. He taught me the value of sealing a deal quickly. We told the agent we were in a position to put down a 5 per cent deposit and sign a contract as soon as possible.

When I took the time to pick his brains I discovered Dad knew a lot more about negotiating deals and obtaining finance than I had realised. With his help and encouragement, I negotiated a purchase price that was almost 20 per cent below the original asking price.

Sometimes we don't become aware of how much those around us know on a given subject until we open our minds and start asking different questions. My Dad had always been around; I just hadn't realised he knew so much.

> *The more you nurture your ego and build your self-confidence, the easier it is to discover the hidden potential in others*

The thrill of the chase

As we settled into our new home, my serial renovator began to work his magic and the house transformed from an ugly duckling into a beautiful swan. Reading about real estate investing further stimulated my interest and broadened my understanding of the main concepts as well as opening my mind to the complexities of the subject.

Books by Robert Kiyosaki such as *Rich Dad Poor Dad* and *Cashflow Quadrant* presented the concept that the rich don't work for money but have money work for them. This was exactly what the psychologist had alluded to at the abundance workshop when she identified the smallest *sliver of pie*.

Seeing the value of crunching numbers Simon and I began to more acutely assess the outgoings and rental returns of our existing properties. We also took time to take stock and appreciate what we had already achieved. When we looked back at the purchase of our former home we realised we had bought it 38 per cent below the original asking price. The vendor had been asking way too much at the time, considering its poor condition. But in less than three years, with Simon's toil, some inexpensive renovations and a little market growth, the place had regained more than 38 per cent in value. We had stumbled onto something good.

Although we were working hard our real estate ventures didn't seem like work—they were more like a hobby. On Saturdays we looked at houses for sale in our local area, enjoying the thrill of the chase, searching for the next great deal.

House hunting brought back memories of looking at houses with my mother when I was a child. I remembered one particular house that made me cringe. When we left the house, I asked her "We're not going to buy that one are we?" She sighed and said it had potential. "But it had ugly carpet and the wallpaper was coming off," I argued. I still remember her reply: "Oh, that's just cosmetics."

The red and gold room

A regal pattern of bright red velour and shiny gold dominated the walls. A heavy timber dining setting sat on the dark chocolate-coloured carpet. Lime green curtains overlaid with purple netting hung across the windows adding the finishing touch to a room that was like nothing else I had ever seen.

With my brain on overload I left the room and went on to inspect other areas of the house. The other rooms, although a little less startling to the eye, were also full of dated and mismatched décor.

Having lived in four houses in less than four years of marriage, Simon and I were developing a growing passion for house renovation. So far each house had been our home but now we were looking to take it further by buying a house purely as an investment. We planned to buy something with potential, do it up and sell it. It sounded simple enough but we really didn't know what we were looking for.

Two young real estate agents were stationed in the living room politely chatting to people among a steady stream of Saturday 'open house' browsers. Keen to see the outlook from the back of the house, I sidled over to peek through the closed blinds and was pleasantly surprised to see a lovely view of the mountains. I couldn't understand why the agents hadn't opened up the curtains and blinds to showcase the view.

The house had that musty closed-up smell and I could see that Simon and my daughter had seen enough and were heading out the front door. I was about to follow when something made me go back and take another look at the red and gold-wallpapered room.

It was even more off-putting at the second take. I wondered what had made me want to take another look. But something made me linger. I stood inside the room and noticed people's reactions as they came in. Most walked out promptly, few staying for more than a few moments. I took another sweeping glance around the house and headed for the car. My daughter declared that it must be the ugliest house in town. Simon agreed but I wasn't so sure.

This house needed a lot of work. My family were standing at the car ready to go but again something was telling me this was worth more consideration. It was a four bedroom, two bathroom house in a very good location. I asked Simon a question. If the house was structurally sound and most of the work was just cosmetic, what would it take in terms of money and time to fix it? This got him thinking. He went back for a second look.

We didn't put in an offer that day. We waited and watched. Over several weeks the house dropped in price. A friend commented what a great street it was in, so we drove up and down looking at the other houses. He was right. The vast majority of the homes in the street were very nice, some even quite grand.

With my ever-improving negotiation skills we eventually bought the property at around 23 per cent below the original asking price. With quite a lot of elbow grease and about four weeks of working long hours, Simon and I completed the renovation and put the house up for sale. Failing to achieve our target price, we decided instead to hold it and rent it out. The property doubled in value within four years.

My hunch to linger in that red and gold room had paid off. I had seen how off-putting that room had been to others and how it had affected my family in the same way. Beneath the garish colours lay a good solid house. With a lick of paint and new carpet, the place began to transform. As my mother had alluded years before, cosmetic renovations can make a big difference.

Intuition saves time and energy

As we continued to look for deals, I became quicker at deciding whether a place had the potential we were looking for. I was learning to trust in those moments when I **knew** something but was not sure why I knew it. There were times when I walked into a house and felt good about it straight away.

The reasoning behind some of my snap judgements may lie hidden in my subconscious mind but for me it is not important where the reasoning or knowledge comes from. I've learned that trusting my gut feelings can save me a lot of time and energy. Although I sometimes enjoy spending time weighing things up, analysing and evaluating I also appreciate occasions when I rely on my inner guidance to make snap decisions thereby giving more time for other things.

The story of the red and gold room was a great example of one of my lucky hunches but this next story is of a time when I was way too busy and preoccupied to be intuitive and the result provided yet another learning curve.

The million-dollar toilet

The tenants were gone but memories of them lingered. Broken furniture lay strewn under the carport and tall weeds waved in the breeze as we walked up the driveway. My hopes were raised as I entered the house and the smell of disinfectant wafted up the hallway only to be shattered as I stepped into a living room strewn with rubbish.

Less than a year before I had decided I would self-manage our investment properties. A good friend, who had been in property management for several years, had mentioned that tenant selection was an important part of the overall process. I was now wishing I had paid closer attention to her advice. I had accepted the first applicants and they had proved to be less than ideal from the start. They had been regularly behind in their rent and had now left the property dirty and in a poor state of repair.

Apart from the rubbish removal, gardening and cleaning required, there were broken light fittings, doors off hinges, stains on the carpet and a range of little things that needed repairing or replacing.

To further add to our exasperation, in my inexperience I had advertised the house "open for inspection" later that morning. We had less than two hours to pull the house into shape before people arrived to look through.

Too late to book a cleaner, I phoned home to elicit the services of some of our kids who were usually happy to lend a hand and earn some quick pocket money. I bolted home and returned a short time later armed with four teenagers, a vacuum, mop, bucket, brooms, rubber gloves and cleaning products.

My next job was to delegate. Tasks were set and the working bee began. I had no sooner headed off to clean the bathroom when a scream emitted from one of the bedrooms. We all ran in to look. Among the nasty debris littering the floor were soiled contraceptive devices. I promptly took charge of the area and set my horrified young teen another less gruesome task.

That job finished, I had just enough time to attack the main bathroom and toilet. I put someone to work scrubbing the scum off the tiles in the shower recess and went to inspect the smallest room in the house. I'd been holding it all together pretty well up til then but now it was my turn to scream and run from the scene.

The smell of disinfectant had once again fooled me. The state of the little room made me cringe. I found Simon and asked him if he could take over. He rattled off a list of heavy-duty chores he needed to complete before he could come to my assistance. It was looking like his princess was going to have to do some dirty work.

Holding my breath and with my eyes half closed I grabbed the cleaner and brush and attacked the offensive utility, scrubbing with gusto. I wanted to get out of there as fast as possible. I was starting to feel angry now.

Why was I doing this? Was it all worth it? I was thinking that being a property investor was seriously overrated.

Overcome by fumes from the cleaning products, I stepping back into the hallway to catch my breath. I realised it had been a busy year. I was working full-time and we'd bought and renovated four more investment properties. It was again timely for me to take stock and appreciate where we had come from. We had recently achieved our first million dollars in equity. As this realisation washed over me, appreciation began to flood through me leaving no room for the anger and frustration I had felt only moments before. I laughed at myself. Would I rather not have all this property and not have put myself in this situation? So what, poor me, I had to clean a poxy toilet. But this toilet suddenly represented a million dollars.

By the time people arrived to inspect, the place was looking quite presentable. We thanked our wonderful workers. I was grateful to have had them on the job. It could have been a lot worse and I decided I would put in place some better property management procedures and planning so as to avoid this type of experience in the future.

Before I left the house I took one last look at the little room and smiled.

It is easy to get so carried away with the thrill of the chase that you forget to appreciate where you've come from, just as it is easy to become sidetracked with frustration when things don't go according to plan. Whenever I look for an upside to any situation I find one. There is hidden potential for a bright side at every turn. Every cloud does have a silver lining. If ever I fail to see it, I know I'm just not looking hard enough.

As Simon and I continued to look at houses we trained ourselves to look for concealed beauty. We learned to look past overgrown gardens and see beyond old or outdated decor. As well as ensuring that the numbers stacked up, we bought properties based on how they felt. With practice we got better at making quick decisions about the type of people we wanted to do business with and the type of properties we wanted to buy. We often saw opportunity where others saw risk; we saw potential in places where others would not think to look.

A diamond in the rough

"Is this it?" The photographer looked perplexed as he looked at the duplex and back at us. He was obviously expecting something a little more sensational. I laughed and confirmed that this was indeed the property he had come to photograph.

A property magazine was running an article on us and this duplex, which was to be featured in the article, was indeed no oil painting. Although recently renovated, it was not particularly attractive or elegant looking and was not about to win any design awards. From the street it was just an ordinary looking residence that had recently been painted and had a garden makeover. I don't know what this photographer had been told about us or about the property, but neither Simon nor I nor the duplex were looking like a million dollars. We were all looking pretty ordinary. If the photographer had seen (or smelt) the property before Simon had worked his magic on it he would have been horrified. It had been a very sad and sorry sight indeed and had smelled so bad the agent refused to accompany us inside when we first went to look at it. The tenant had kept the place closed up with several animals living inside.

The weather was cold, drizzly and blustery so I had abandoned the idea of an alluring shot of me in the sunshine wearing something glamorous. Instead I appeared in layers of clothes with windswept hair and chattering teeth. The photographer had been liaising with me by phone as we waited for a break in the weather, but with a deadline to meet we had no choice but to proceed. The icy wind persisted but the rain had finally eased so we had agreed to meet at the property and take our chances.

This property was another classic example of hidden potential— a diamond in the rough. It looked ordinary from the street but it was our best money-spinner yet. The purchase price was way below market value and the return on investment was exceptional when both the rental return and improved capital value after renovation were taken into account.

When people read the article and assessed the deal they could see what a great example this was of how you can make money from residential real estate. But if you were to only look at the photo of Simon and I with our ordinary looking duplex in the background, you would wonder what all the fuss was about.

Just as it is true that all that glitters is not gold, many people will walk past something precious because they don't see its real value. We are surrounded by people and places that are loaded with hidden potential. Our world is full of unpolished gems.

12

Perfect world

Enhancing your ability to see your world the way you want it to be

Some neighbours have a front doorbell that seems to activate their kettle. My next-door neighbour, Erica, was one of those neighbours. I'd ring the bell and before I knew it I'd have a welcoming cup of tea in my hands and stimulating conversation would be well under way.

Erica is a psychologist and works as a counsellor in high schools. Erica and I didn't get together very often but whenever we did I always felt uplifted. When I first met Erica we both had teenagers, so discussing issues around living with and understanding teenagers was often on our agenda. Her insight and compassion made me glad that there are people like her in our world, offering encouragement and support to young ones at a significant phase of their development.

Erica has a wonderful habit of listening patiently and responding with questions that help me to find my own answers. She told me of a question she sometimes asked her clients.

If you were to wake up tomorrow to a perfect world, what would you see?

I found the perfect world question so powerful I tried it out on some of my friends. Some interpreted it in a broader sense. One friend said a perfect world to her would be achieving world peace. Although her vision was understandable I wanted the question to be more personal. I wanted people to think more about their own world. The world they have the power to change right now. As Stephen Covey describes in his book *Seven Habits of Highly Effective People*, **focus on your circle of influence**. That's where our real power lies.

Changing one word in the sentence brings the focus back to your circle of influence rather than your circle of concern.

If you were to wake up tomorrow to YOUR perfect world, what would you see?

The perfect world question helps to identify areas of your life that are worthy of renewed focus. For example, if like my friend, you desire world peace, concentrate on fostering harmony in the world that surrounds you. Nurture the relationships you already have and aim to continually improve your own ability to get along with others.

The idea is to continue to find new things that you like and better ways of doing things that you already do. While *The Launching Pad* exercise is designed to shift you from a negative to a positive focus, *The Perfect World* exercise aims to foster personal growth and is best practiced when you are feeling good. A good starting point is to take the opportunity to appreciate the elements of perfection that already exist in the world that surrounds you.

Some may think that it is greedy to want lots of nice new things or experiences. But why place a judgement on your, or anyone else's, appetite for enjoyment? The *perfect world* exercise is about recognising the abundance life has to offer and utilising every opportunity you can, to grow and flourish. It requires an understanding that our world is plentiful to those who allow themselves to appreciate all that is on offer. It is through our own willingness to thrive that we inspire others to do the same. It's funny how perfect the world can look when you keep on looking for things that make you happy.

My perfect world

The perfect world question stimulated my mind. It made me think about every aspect of my life. I pictured myself waking up next to my husband and hearing my kids rattling around in the kitchen getting their breakfast. I had a lot to appreciate. I was happily married with a wonderful family and a nice home. There were a lot of things about my life that I liked. But I was irritated that I had to go off to work in a rush and was rarely at home to greet my kids when they came home from school. I still felt frustrated that I was letting an employer dictate how I spent such a large portion of my time. I decided it was time for a holiday. As soon as we could organise time off work, I booked flights and a beachfront resort on the Gold Coast.

Holiday heaven

The winds had reached gale force making conditions on the beach hellish for holiday makers. In fact, walking anywhere outdoors was becoming increasing unpleasant. The first couple of days had been great. Simon and I had been enjoying time at the beach. But now the blustery weather had cleared the streets that were normally bustling with tourists.

Shopping provided some relief while we waited for the weather to improve and we discovered a quirky bookstore only a block from our resort. I had recently read a book by Robert Kiyosaki wherein he recommended Napoleon Hill's Think and Grow Rich. *It felt serendipitous that this was one of the first books I saw when I entered the bookshop.*

With perfect weather for reading, I abandoned my vision of a dream beach holiday and curled up on the sofa to read this timeless classic.

Although the secret of Think and Grow Rich *seemed to elude me, I couldn't help but feel that I'd stumbled on to something special.*

As I lost myself among the pages, I felt I had escaped into another world, where my imagination was allowed to run free with no restrictions. The rules that applied to my normal routine existence didn't apply here. Despite wild weather I had entered a place I now refer to as 'Holiday Heaven'.

The marvellous thing about *Holiday Heaven* is that you don't actually have to go on a holiday to get into this state of mind. The main objective is to pursue opportunities to break from routine and relax so that you can allow yourself to become more open-minded and think more expansively. I have discovered that thinking big comes more easily when I'm relaxed.

Holidays can, however, provide an ideal opportunity to lose yourself and find yourself. I got lost in the pages of the book and found something special, something unexpected; a chance to take stock and think about what was really important to me. Having removed myself from the accountability and regimentation of my commitments, I felt more relaxed. I had temporarily escaped from the influences of society that made me feel I should conform and 'think' or 'act' in a predictable or mainstream way. Removing time pressure to 'get things done' allowed space for my creative mind to flourish.

Holidays give us an opportunity to get our life back on track or take a new direction; a chance to reflect on things about our life that we really treasure; a time to make big changes or solve problems. Holidays give you a window of opportunity to lose that part of yourself that worries about the less appealing realities of your current situation and find the part of yourself who can imagine a bigger, better and brighter future. Whether you are going away to relax or going on an adventure, a holiday gives you a chance to view your life from a different perspective so that you can dare to think big enough to embrace significant change.

Fourteen months to financial freedom

Following my experience in *Holiday Heaven,* I was thriving. I came back home so fired-up with enthusiasm to effect change, I made up my mind to follow advice I had read in many self-help books including *Think and Grow Rich*. I felt compelled to put my goal in writing.

Putting my thoughts on paper gave me greater clarity and a definiteness of purpose, which helped me to focus and prioritise much more easily. It prompted me to add detail and more specific information that supported my big picture.

Mind mapping or drawing pictures

Because we are all different, we don't all respond to the same set of instructions. I found it beneficial to experiment with different ways of expressing what I want on paper.

Mind-mapping is another exercise I enjoy and it works best when you're open-minded. A simple take on it is to take pen to paper and write down your major idea or focus and draw a circle around it (like a bubble). Then write ideas, tasks, plans or directives that flow from or link to that central focus. A mind map can be useful in organising information and can have the effect of stimulating the creative part of your mind.

Another exercise that I learnt while involved in network marketing was to draw a picture of your dream or goal. At a workshop I attended, the presenter suggested that we draw a picture or image of what we want *without using words.* This may sound easy but I found it quite challenging and enormously thought provoking.

At the time I was living in Canberra, an inland city with a population of around 340,000. Although we enjoyed a lovely mountain view from our home, the lure of beachside living was very strong. This exercise proved to be unbelievably powerful as I'm now living what I drew then.

The picture I drew was of a house just up the hill from a beautiful beach. At first it was secluded, just sitting on the hill on its own but then I realised that I wanted to be around people so I drew other big houses around it. I drew aeroplanes flying high in the background. This represented a busy airport nearby. I then drew lots of people because, as I sketched, I realised that I craved the thump of the big city where entertainment and travel are easy options.

I now live in Sydney on Balmoral slopes in an idyllic location. I love the convenience of being only a 12-minute ferry ride from the city and a half-hour drive to the airport. I can easily jump on a plane to just about anywhere in the world but I always love coming home to this fabulous place.

Three powerful processes

The following three strategies had a huge impact on launching me along a path to financial success:

- Putting goals in writing (or drawing a picture or mind-map)
- Positive self-talk
- Visualisation

The impact of utilising these three processes was so huge it is hard for me to express their immense value in words. For years I had yearned to break free of the bonds of working for a wage and these three processes helped me to achieve my dream in just 14 months. Then, I was able to quit my job and leave paid employment behind. I will explain my take on this in more detail, as it is important to approach this in the right frame of mind.

Are your ideas fixed or flexible?

The stories in *Think and Grow Rich* reinforced my ideas about embracing new possibilities rather than getting bogged down with self-limiting beliefs or society's view of what is possible. Our world is laden with examples of extraordinary human achievement and yet we are not all stimulated by these things in the same way or at the same time.

When the idea of speed reading was introduced to me it was not a new concept, but the confidence my friend emanated, and the enthusiasm she shared that day, fuelled my desire to implement change. Our minds are more likely to become open when we are inspired or motivated towards change. Fixed beliefs about my potential to generate income were slowly dissolving, making way for the flexible thinking that would make me wealthy.

Little shifts towards big change

The best time to embrace change is when your mind is flexible and open. I used to think that effecting big change was all about hard work and perseverance. But I now realise it is hard work to try and use willpower against a stubborn belief or habit. It is much easier and much less work to introduce a new idea or expectation that comfortably replaces your old belief. I use the word *comfortably* in the sense that it must be a conceivable shift for you. Rather than expecting your mind to make an extreme leap of faith it is easier to introduce new ideas that line up with your big picture in a way that is *comfortable* for you. This way you can make a series of little shifts that will still take you towards the significant change you want and the results will be more permanent and lasting. Appreciate every win along the way, no matter how small, as this will fuel your positive energy and carry you naturally to more success.

Positive self-talk and affirmations will only work in line with your beliefs. For example, if I had made an affirmation, "I make large sums of money easily and quickly" yet my underlying belief was that "making large sums of money in a short time could be fraught with risk" my belief would have generated fear that would have undermined my desire. In order to feel more comfortable with making larger sums of money, I shifted my beliefs gradually, and my outcomes improved with each change.

Big shifts are also possible in a short time when your mind is open and fear is not inhibiting your progress. An example of this was when I was younger and wanted to give up smoking.

No butts about it

"Let's rip them up into little pieces and throw them in the bin," suggested Linda. I agreed that this supreme act of destruction would surely be enough to curb our addiction. Linda and I were teenagers, still at college and cigarettes were expensive, especially as we were students without much spare cash.

Linda and I had tried making pacts together. We'd tried not buying any, but ended up smoking other people's. We tried for months to give up smoking. We partied together, laughed together, smoked together and coughed together. We were fed up and frustrated. Why was this so hard? I remember sitting in her bedroom as we ceremoniously pulled each cigarette apart, extracting every last string of tobacco and tearing the paper and butts to bits. We'd tried using sheer willpower but it seemed it wasn't enough. Surely destroying the last of our cigarettes would do it. We normally decided we would give up at the end of a pack but this seemed like a significant act to us. It would be a waste of both money and willpower if we caved in after this.

To cut a long story short, Linda and I didn't give up smoking after our cigarette destruction ceremony. But not long after that my Dad heard about a local hypnotherapist who specialised in helping people give up smoking. I went to one session and it worked. The session was called 'The last cigarette' and for me it certainly was. The cigarette I smoked in that session all those years ago was indeed the last cigarette I ever smoked.

How was it possible that I could give up smoking in one session and yet months of endeavouring to use sheer willpower had failed? The answer is so simple and it does not require hard work, perseverance or any significant pain. It just required a shift in my belief system. Let me explain.

While I was trying to give up cigarettes with Linda, my brain was programmed with a pleasure mechanism attached to the action of smoking. Whenever I lit up a cigarette, I enjoyed the sensation. But when I developed a bad cough, I decided I wanted to give up. The problem was that a part of my brain was not prepared to give up the pleasure, regardless of any associated pain.

Even though I had a belief that said 'smoking is bad for my health' a stronger urge to experience the pleasure I received took over, as if I was out of control. The brilliant thing that the therapist did was that he reprogrammed my brain by suggesting to me, under hypnosis, that the taste of cigarettes was abhorrent to me. He went into great detail describing how bad cigarettes now tasted to me. He spoke for a couple of hours and I do not recall all that he said but the major shift he managed to help me to accomplish was that cigarettes were no longer pleasant. He took away the pleasure and replaced it with pain; the pain of having an ugly taste overriding what used to be a pleasant experience.

As the session name suggested, he reached a point where he asked everyone in the group to light up a cigarette and he told us it would taste vile. He also told us it would be the last cigarette we would ever smoke.

*I went from believing that smoking was something that gave me pleasure to believing that smoking was something that tasted so foul it could only be an unpleasant experience. He shifted my belief **big time**, in the space of a couple of hours. My new belief was that 'smoking tastes terrible and is an unpleasant experience'. After that day, I still experienced cravings for a while but my new belief would pop into my head and I'd think 'Well there's no point. I've given up now and it would taste terrible anyway.'*

The therapist who conducted this session had a great success rate but his strategy did not work for everyone. I later met people who told me that they had attended a similar session and yet continued to smoke. So what was different about them and me? It is most likely because I was incredibly open-minded about the experience and eager to effect change. I had made a definite decision to give up and I *expected* that this therapy would work.

Using sheer willpower to effect change is hard work. Shifting your beliefs and adopting a new expectation is a much easier road.

Written affirmations

Think of a written affirmation as a statement describing how you would like things to be. Our self-talk is very powerful yet there is enormous added benefit in writing down what you want. Writing brings clarity of focus that will add power to your intention.

You can think of it as an exercise in putting *your perfect world* in writing. Call it a goal, a plan or a desire—what you call it is not important, what is important is that you understand the advantage of writing it down.

When I first discovered this concept, I kept it simple and started small. I began with a sentence or two and then built on it. I'd write out an affirmation I felt comfortable with and repeated it in my mind. Your affirmations need to be things that are meaningful to you: a statement of what you want or who you wish to become. You also can write affirmations in the present tense as if you have already achieved them. For example, if I were to write *I have a great memory and easily remember people's names,* I remove my focus from any recent slip-ups and instead focus on what I want: *a great* memory. Writing the statement in the present tense creates a new expectation: that I will remember details and names because I am acknowledging that I am now better utilising the great memory I was born with.

Before you read on, you may be tempted to gloss over these words. But I want you to stop and consider the power of the written word or of drawing an image on paper. It is one thing to think something, another thing again to say it or 'verbalise it' and a further commitment again to put your thoughts on paper.

The best time to do this is when you are relaxed and happy with where you are and yet excited and eager for more. Take a pen and paper and write a description or draw an image of *your perfect world*.

Be relaxed and easy about it and remember, this is meant to be fun! Write about something you would like to improve, a positive change you would like to see occurring in your life. Focus on any area of your life, for example: home, work, social, mind, body or spirit. If you decide to draw a picture, instead of using words, make sure that your picture only contains things that are desirable to you. You are looking to find perfection in your world so unwanted things have no place in your picture.

If you are using words, be clear about what you want. Write about why you want these things and how your life will be better when you have them. Write some of the reasons why you believe you will have these things. Will others be better off with your improved circumstances? How will the attainment of your desires make you feel?

Positive self-talk

The thing about self-talk is that we all do it. Notice what you are saying to yourself. How much of it is positive? The time it takes to adopt positive or useful thoughts is minimal and the rewards can be immeasurable. Leaving your mind on autopilot, makes your life a game of chance rather than having it flow in the direction of your choosing.

It is estimated that we generate many thousands of thoughts every day. That gives us thousands of opportunities each day to think upbeat thoughts and make positive statements to ourselves. Think of it like taking your mind to the gym. You can give your body a workout, why not your mind? The more you work your mind the fitter it becomes.

Program your mind to work *for you* not against you. When I began to repeat simple affirmations in my head on a regular basis my self-talk became more positive, more refined and more powerful as I gathered momentum. When you repeat affirmations in your head often enough the new belief or expectation eventually comes so naturally to you that you become it automatically.

Because we create self-fulfilling prophecies from our thoughts, the quality of our self-talk can make the difference between setting ourselves up for self-sabotage or adopting a recipe for success.

Visualisation

Find time when you can clear your mind and escape from reality long enough to picture *Your Perfect World*. How will your life be better?

Get relaxed and be open-minded. Picture your desire in your mind, have fun with it and run a movie in your head where you are the star. You are playing the leading role and you can be as clever, talented, popular or successful as you would like to be. The good feelings you generate from this experience help to put you in a positive emotional state. It is important to picture what you want, not the lack of it. Use your imagination to picture your perfect world scenario as if you have already achieved it.

There is no need to spend too long on this. Five or 10 minutes a few times a week works better than a half hour session once a week. The reason for this is that it is best to stop before you hit problems or it gets too complicated. Visualisation is not about trouble shooting or imagining things that *might* go wrong. It is all about seeing things the way you want them to be.

Relax your mind and engage that wonderfully powerful imagination you were born with. Experiment with pictures and scenarios that excite and stimulate you and turn your attention elsewhere when your visualisation loses its positive momentum.

Change provides opportunity for improvement

The contrast in our life is what makes our life stimulating and interesting. We balance our way through, embracing what we like and discarding what we dislike, while all the time acknowledging that our world is constantly changing and expanding. We can resist change in the short term but in the long run it is much easier to keep moving and remain flexible and open-minded as the variety and diversity of our existence continues to prod and poke at our sensibilities. Every (perceived) negative change provides opportunity for improvement. How soon you create the opportunity is up to you. When you move forward with an open mind and an active imagination with a view to developing clear intentions coupled with positive expectations you are lining yourself up for a more perfect world. You can't *make* other's lives perfect, but by improving your own lot, you encourage and inspire others to do the same.

Change stimulates new desires, and when you disregard probabilities and focus on possibilities, you can identify what you want based *purely* on what you desire, rather than based on your past achievements or your current reality.

Much of the work in achieving any great measure of success lies in our ability to imagine our goal has already been achieved. And this is an ongoing process that will become more powerful as you continue to practice it.

- *Imagine waking up tomorrow to your Perfect World. How will your life be better?*
- *Put pen to paper and write or draw a picture of your Perfect World*
- *Visualise your Perfect World, as if it has already been achieved*

No perfect words or actions – just a perfect picture

In seeking to achieve financial freedom, Simon and I drafted plans to achieve our goal. We wrote out affirmations and drew up a business plan. Now I look back on our written goals and plans and realise that it was not so much the words that we wrote but the feelings those words generated within us.

Some people think they need to come up with the perfect plan. The truth is there is no such thing as a perfect plan or a perfect world. What really matters is how you feel about your world. If drawing up a plan and writing affirmations is going to build your confidence and make you feel good, feel excited, feel enthusiastic, then you are on track. If you draw up a plan or write or recite words that overwhelm you or scare you it will be harder for you to stay on your path.

Our thoughts and feelings go hand in hand. Search for the combinations of words and thoughts that generate the right feelings within you. Gathering knowledge is only useful if it builds your confidence and makes you feel good about the direction you are heading in. Sometimes we gather information only to find that the thing we thought we wanted doesn't look so good when we get closer to it.

Property felt right for Simon and I. We became excited about it and about the prospect of making money from it. We didn't have perfect plans but we did have a perfect vision.

Powerful partnerships

Bringing out the strength in others so they shine on your parade

The meaning of financial freedom

Imagine you were to achieve something so significant, so life-changing, that you clearly remember the day when you made up your mind that you were going to do it. You remember the moment you made that decision, the sequence of events that led you to that *aha* moment, that point of **knowing** that you could do it no matter what others thought about what you were capable of, no matter what others thought about the probability of your success. The moment you knew you could do it because the passion and enthusiasm within you wouldn't accept anything else? That's how I feel about the day I *decided* I would achieve financial freedom.

I have heard the terms *financial freedom* and *financial independence* used quite loosely, so it is important to be clear on what it is I wanted to achieve. To explain what I mean by *financial freedom* I will quote from Robert Kiyosaki's book *Rich Dad, Poor Dad*. "The poor and the middle class work for money. The rich have money work for them."

In my book, if you **have to** work for a wage or work in your own business, you are not financially independent. Financial freedom comes from creating passive income streams, so that you have plenty of money to support your lifestyle whether or not you are working, and this allows you greater freedom to control your time and your income.

A joint vision

Fired up with an intention to effect substantial positive change, I sat down with pen and paper and began to write. Writing about what I wanted felt good but there was something missing. I stopped. It occurred to me that this exercise would have much greater impact if Simon and I did it together. I knew that building a joint vision would hold even greater power.

With this in mind, Simon and I arranged a time when the kids were otherwise occupied so that we could discuss our plans without interruption. It wasn't very formal. We sat on sofas in the living room and after some discussion we took pen to paper. We each drew up a draft plan of what we wanted to achieve in terms of both our rental income and portfolio growth. We did this exercise separately, sitting across from one another, and then swapped sheets to compare notes. We felt it was important that we each have the opportunity to draft up a plan without the influence of the other, before we pooled our ideas.

After comparing notes, we agreed on a target figure and timeframe for its achievement. The exercise left us both feeling excited and committed. We had made a definite decision to *go for it*; to achieve financial freedom *and* we had **put it in writing**.

This was our first real business meeting and it was to be the first of many. It was memorable because it gave us a strong and clear joint focus that made it easier to streamline our thoughts. Without a clear focus there is more potential to dissipate your energy in different directions. At this time I was happy with the other areas of my life and aimed to maintain a status quo while at the same time keeping my eye on the prize.

Powerful planning

My memory of this meeting is still crystal clear in my mind. It brought about a major positive change in our relationship. We were very happy together but this was the first time we had sat and **planned** together with a bigger picture in mind. We had already bought property together, renovated and rented properties out. We had made many smaller decisions together, but the difference now was making the big decision to significantly grow our portfolio to a particular level in a projected timeframe.

Following this meeting we agreed to meet on a regular basis to review our plans and plot our progress. In amongst working, raising a family and running a household we needed to allocate time when we could think about business and devote time to focusing on our financial target.

We hit a hurdle on one occasion when our bank refused to loan us money for another investment property because we were 'too rent reliant'. Undeterred, we found a pro forma business plan on the internet that we completed and presented to another bank. They approved our loan in record time. Developing a business plan reaffirmed our focus and boosted our self-confidence when we realised that we were already covering many of the bases that were suggested in the pro forma. It provided further opportunity to refine our strategy and gave us credibility when we approached banks for further investment loans.

Ten things I love about you

With our relationship expanding from a marriage to a business partnership, I decided it would be prudent to look at what we were both bringing to the table.

What skills and attributes did we each have to offer that would help us achieve our financial goal?

Again we sat with paper and pen, and this time I suggested we each write 10 things that we admired about the other. We listed positive personality traits and the skills we perceived would be each other's strengths in business.

This exercise helped us to define areas where we could lean on each other's strong points. As our portfolio grew we got better at bringing out the best in each other. It has made working together on an ongoing basis enjoyable because we are clear about what we each have to offer. We encourage each other's creativity and ability to think beyond the obvious.

We did not look for any perceived weakness in one another. We only looked for strength. With a positive focus, we seemed to naturally cover all of the bases for managing and growing our portfolio. Simon is creative and hard-working and can quickly work his way through a big renovation project, doing a vast majority of the work himself. He's also great at accounting. I enjoy dealing with people, looking at the big picture and making decisions. We found ways to complement one another's traits, skills and leanings. The more we look for strength and talent in each other, the more we find it.

Another perspective

It seems apt that I include my partner's take on this. Below are things Simon liked about doing the exercise **10 things I love about you**, even though he does not share my propensity for putting things in writing.

- There were things I said that were surprising to him; things that opened doors of potential in his mind
- It helped reinforce some of the things he loves about me
- It re-affirmed the harmony in our relationship and gave us a strong grounding from which to move forward

Happy with who you are

This is a simple yet powerful exercise for potential partners but it is important to recognise the emotional standpoint from which Simon and I approached this. When I met Simon I was happy with myself. I was not looking for someone to make me complete. I just wanted a partner I could harmonise with. Simon also was happy within himself and easy going. I found him to be free thinking and fun to be with. He encouraged me to follow my dreams.

One night at a dinner we met a couple who had been married for over 20 years. The husband was easy to be around as he had a gentle *allowing* nature and a dry wit. But I found his wife frustrating. She spent more time complaining than she did admiring. She whinged about many things: her job, her health, her family, and especially her husband. I would not suggest this exercise to someone like her while she is so unhappy with herself and while she continues to find fault in so many of the things she observes.

That is why it is important to build on your own strengths and self-confidence. When you are happy with yourself it is much easier to find happiness with another. When you can easily write 10 things you love about yourself, writing 10 things you love about someone you are close to will be an enjoyable and powerful exercise.

If you want put your own slant on it and start on a smaller scale, start with five or three. Even three things you can admire about each other is a great basis to work from. It is a beneficial exercise for couples, regardless of financial goals, as you can do it for fun to strengthen your relationship.

The rind of the bacon

During the first few years of our marriage the Gold Coast was a favourite family holiday destination and Simon and I enjoyed browsing the real estate agency windows and chatting to local agents. On one of our trips we struck up a conversation with a man who had a substantial holding of real estate in the area. When I asked him what suburbs he recommended, he didn't hesitate. "There's only one place to buy on the Gold Coast and that's the rind of the bacon." His reply was crisp and his message clear. "People want to live on the coastline. Buy right on the beach or as close to it as you can."

When Canberra's market began to rise in 2001, we decided to look further afield. We decided to take a look at the Gold Coast as our research indicated that prices in the area had remained relatively static for almost 10 years. We spent a week looking at numerous properties and talking further with local agents. We narrowed our selection down to two properties. One was a house on a hill in a pleasant suburb only a short distance from Surfers Paradise Beach. The other was a unit on the beachfront at Bilinga.

After we weighed up the pros and cons of each property, we made our final decision with a quirky phrase sticking in our mind, 'the rind of the bacon'. We decided to buy on the beach. We liked the location and our timing was good. The market was ripe for a boom. It turned out to be ideal because the property tripled in value within six years.

The Gold Coast unit was our seventh purchase together and is an example of why our partnership works so well. We constantly search for opportunities to harmonise our desires, both get what we want and both be happy. I crave variety and can become frustrated if I stay in one place for too long. I like to keep moving so I don't get bored—with myself or with what is around me. To me the biggest deadly sin is not being interesting.

Having bought six properties together in Canberra I was itching to branch out. Looking in an area that was less familiar was exciting for me. I met new people and explored a different environment.

Simon loves strategising. He was happy to consider the Gold Coast as long as the numbers stacked up. When we did our research, Simon was satisfied that the purchase was a good choice at that time.

The power of more than one

People in powerful partnerships communicate regularly and devote time to reviewing and refining plans as their joint vision takes shape. The bigger the goal the more often you will need to discuss and hone your strategy as you progress. I've spoken to couples who have set a goal six or 12 months previously yet rarely meet to discuss it. Notice I used the word *meet*. If you are living with someone day in day out it is easy to fall into the trap of assuming that you are both heading in the same direction. Without regular focused communication you can lose touch with each other on a particular subject. You can't and won't both think and feel exactly the same on any given subject but it can be exciting to aim at a mutual target together, especially when you tune into the same wavelength and allow your different perspectives to add strength to your joint vision.

New expectations

In the past Simon and I had thought debt was bad. Now we were learning the value of using other people's money to make more money. It was not like consumer debt where people borrow for lifestyle. We were focused on a strategy that would create wealth through leverage. We used borrowed money to make more money by acquiring income-producing, appreciating assets with a view to enjoying a lifestyle that was free from financial stress. In order to achieve this Simon and I had to replace old beliefs about money with new expectations **no matter how unrealistic they were to others**.

Terrific targets

When it comes to setting goals and targets, whether you are working on your own or in a partnership you want to aim at something that you feel comfortable with. Understand the *balance* between thinking big and wanting to extend yourself yet not feeling overwhelmed by what may seem to you to be an unrealistic dream.

Only you can be the judge of what is right for you. Don't let anyone tell you your goals are too big and unrealistic or too modest or small. How much is too much? Only you can know and the best indicator is how you feel about it. If you feel excited every time you think about it then you're on the right track. If it scares you more than excites you then perhaps you can scale it down or shift your focus to something that does push your buttons. Fear will make you shrink. Excitement and enthusiasm will cause you to seek opportunities for expansion and exploration. No matter what your goal you want it to be an enjoyable experience so you can have fun along the way.

The emotional connection needs to be a positive one fuelled by excitement or else it will be in danger of being extinguished by fear or frustration. You are much more likely to achieve your terrific target if you are enjoying the journey.

Do what *feels* right and don't let your brain get in the way too much. If you over analyse everything and try to make it all perfect before you begin you'll never get started. I didn't worry *how* I was going to achieve my goal. I just believed it was possible and I continually *imagined* how good it would *feel* when I didn't have to get up in the morning and go and work for someone else. And for over eight years now I have enjoyed the benefits of achieving that goal. I am normally an early riser but I love knowing that I can sleep in when I feel so inclined and, that when I do get up, it is to attend to my own agenda, doing things that are meaningful to me.

Mutual understanding

Not everyone wants to be the boss or the leader. Some people thrive as second in command; they flourish and perform at their best knowing they don't have to bear the responsibility of being the chief organiser or decision maker. It is only natural that some think big, while others are more laid back.

If you wish to work more effectively with your partner make the effort to understand what makes them tick. What is their personality type? What traits do they have that you can work with and what traits do you have that they may not understand or appreciate? Anything that will help you develop a better understanding of the similarities and differences between yourself and those around you is bound to assist in your quest to work well in a partnership or team.

Establish your co-operative financial strength

As Simon and I grew our property portfolio little by little, we established our financial strength by developing skills that we enjoyed using. In addition to his renovation abilities, Simon does the bookkeeping and manages our accounts. He enjoys forecasting and has spent countless hours drawing up spreadsheets that enable him to assess deals and project our portfolio growth.

My increasing knowledge of property management and my keenness to read *the fine print* added to our expertise. I also learned bargaining techniques from people who negotiate for a living—real estate agents. I have spoken to many agents over the years and learned from the best. My negotiating skills resulted in significant price reductions on properties we purchased.

Understanding your partner's strengths and leanings takes the pressure off feeling that you have to make every decision on your own or do everything yourself. Develop skills that you can enjoy applying to your money-making strategy and team up with others who complement those skills. When you do this, making money can be as much fun as spending it!

> *Add power to your partnership*
> - *Sit with pen and paper, when you are both relaxed and unlikely to be interrupted, and* **plot your joint vision**
> - *Establish each other's strengths by writing* **10 things I love about you**
> - *Discover the power of more than one through* **regular communication and planning**

The master of the two-minute phone call

One real estate agent we had some dealings with had an easy going yet confident air that suggested he was not someone you would mess with. I remember him fondly as the master of the two-minute phone call. He had a knack of saying a lot with only a few words.

He encouraged Simon and I to learn more about property management so we could self-manage our properties and deal directly with tenants ourselves, thereby cutting out the middle man. His advice turned out to be brilliant because taking on the property management resulted in a major turnaround for us. It was the start of a great learning curve and we began to see our tenants as real people instead of names on a lease. We have learned so much since that day and the interaction we have had with our tenants has been one of the most enjoyable parts of our property investing. Our dealings with this agent reminded us of a concept we had read about: the power of the Master Mind.

Making the most of other people's minds

"The 'Master Mind' may be defined as: Coordination of knowledge and effort, in a spirit of harmony, between two or more people, for the attainment of a definite purpose." From *Think and Grow Rich* by Napoleon Hill

Inspired by the concept Napoleon Hill referred to as *The power of the Master Mind*, Simon and I were unsure how to go about finding the right people so it was several years before I formally gathered with others in this way and this story is featured later in the book.

The concept, however, reminded us of the benefits of teaming up with the right people and making the most of other people's minds. I know that the outcomes I achieve when I do this far exceed anything I could accomplish on my own.

Allow others to build success on their terms

Have you ever observed someone on the verge of something significant, some wonderful achievement only to watch them shrink back down to a place where they think their partner, family or friends will feel comfortable with them? It may seem like some people want to keep you from growing or from reaching greater potential. They may pretend they are afraid of seeing you get hurt or falling off your pedestal but they may really be afraid of who you may become in your brilliance because it shows up the lack of theirs.

Allowing someone to hinder you from blossoming does not serve you, just as it does not serve you to hinder another's growth or expansion. A desire to control or manipulate others comes from fear: that those who think or act differently to us pose a threat; that we can't have what we want without the cooperation or inclusion of others.

Some people may lead you to believe that they know 'what is good for you', as if you're not smart enough to know yourself. They may prod or prompt you to follow their version of 'the truth' or the 'right way of doing things' rather than acknowledging that 'your truth' or 'your way' is right for you even though it may appear extremely different to their view. But who are we to judge what others are capable of or to expect others to live life according to our rules? Why is it that people in a society sometimes criticise those who don't comply or conform?

What appears impossible to one may be entirely possible for another. We are not here to size up each other's dreams and hopes and give them a probability rating. We are here to expand our own horizons as much as we dare, to spread our wings and fly into the face of opportunity as we conquer our fear of falling or our fear of failing.

When you allow others to build success on their terms you are operating from a base of confidence. Rather than being fearful, you are stimulated by the diversity of beliefs and ideas of others and excited by positive interactions with people who support you in endeavours that are meaningful to you as you support them in the same way. It doesn't mean that you offer full support to everyone you come across but it does mean that you don't discourage others who may be doing something that doesn't make sense to you. Focus on aligning yourself with people who are on the same wavelength.

Our successes and failures in life are our own doing. We get the best results when we fine-tune what we want rather than *expect* someone else to do it for us. Rather than trying to avoid the *wrong* people, make it your point of focus to align with people whose intentions harmonise with yours; aim to connect with people who support, encourage and nurture you and delight in your success just as you do in theirs.

You can't change other people's minds. The only mind you can change is your own. Your potential to inspire others is greatly increased when you feel good about yourself. The best way to help others is to look for the best in them, while you allow them to connect with the best in you. When Simon and I focused on building a powerful partnership, the rewards were numerous and sometimes surprising, appearing when we least expected them.

Running past the finishing line

Balancing work and play and remembering to have fun

Life is like riding a bicycle. To keep your balance you must keep moving.

Albert Einstein

Recharging your batteries

There is a wonderful energy that forms around people who gather together to share their enjoyment and enthusiasm of a mutual interest or passion. Whether it is a social club or business network, or a sport or hobby, there is nothing quite like the *buzz* you get when you mix with people who share a common interest.

Simon and I have found this *buzz* or energy when we mix with other like-minded property investors. We love sharing stories, laughing over hiccups and applauding each other's success. We have made many great friends in these circles and found that investor meetings have been a great way to network, share ideas and recharge our batteries.

Running past the finishing line

Through our investor network we heard of an educational evening for investors. The speaker had been billed as having extensive experience in both share trading and real estate investment. We decided to attend and became intrigued as the presenter proclaimed the benefits of achieving financial freedom and outlined a strategy that would enable an investor to quit their job and live off their investments.

The presenter drew little houses up on the whiteboard. He wrote a figure next to each house representing its market value. The images on the whiteboard became more complex as his talk progressed. There were figures representing loan amounts, rental returns, loan-to-value ratios and a summary of the amount of equity that could still be drawn down to fund further purchases.

He was giving an example of a couple, Mary and Fred. Simon and I watched in amazement as the presenter wrote up the total value of the portfolio, total equity, cash flow, expenses and projected capital growth on the board.

We couldn't believe our eyes. Our portfolio value, equity and cash flow was worth more than the example.

Our mouths dropped open as the presenter said, "Mary and Fred would be able to quit their jobs and leave paid employment forever!" We felt a bit like little kids who were running in a race but no one had told us where the finish line was. We had accumulated enough assets to quit our jobs and hadn't even realised it!

With our minds abuzz we hardly slept that evening. Fourteen months earlier, when we had set a goal to become financially independent, we thought we had to have rental income that would cover all of our investment expenses as well as our lifestyle costs. We had numerous meetings with this man over the following months and what we learned from him is discussed in greater detail in the following chapter.

Who's controlling your time?

The clincher for us was getting back control of our time. Having money is all very well but we decided it wouldn't be much fun unless we had the time to spend it and enjoy life on our terms.

Achieving a big goal like financial freedom was awesome. The timeframe Simon and I had set for achieving our target was three years and yet we achieved it in just 14 months. I now believe the amount of time it takes depends on how quickly you replace resistant beliefs with positive expectations and how much you want change.

The biggest bonus has been the change to our lifestyle. We suddenly found we were able to spend more time with our family and go on more trips. We had more time to research various real estate markets and were able to devote more time to maintaining and growing our portfolio. We were also now in a position to buy back into the Sydney market which years before had seemed unachievable.

Moments of triumph

Waking up one morning knowing that I didn't have to *go to work* anymore gave me a great sense of freedom. Simon and I were now able to devote more time to things that were exciting to us. We bought a house in Sydney and spent time renovating it.

One of my dreams had been to move back to beautiful Sydney. We bought three more properties in Sydney while we waited for our youngest to finish school. After 15 years away, Sydney was a dream-come-true, especially as I no longer had to contend with peak hour traffic. I could enjoy the beach and the harbour-side walks at my leisure. I love the vast areas of national park and the energy in and around the city centre; I love the diversity of the people and the endless stream of things to see and do.

Pre-programmed to want more

Some people have been so in awe of our achievement of financial freedom they want to know *exactly* how much money we had made and what our portfolio was worth. They ask many questions, searching for *the answer* to their own success. They think that they will become happier when they have more money but, in doing this, they fail to realise that the attainment of our dreams is not the real prize. The true reward comes from our life experience along the way. Our achievements are not as important as who we have become as a result of the journey.

Although this event marked a significant turning point in my life, it was to lead to many more moments of triumph. Those who think that one event will mark a high point in their life are selling themselves short. We are not designed to reach our full potential and then stop or relax for the rest of our lives. That is why I believe the idea of *retirement* is flawed. We are pre-programmed for continuous self-improvement and that is part of the glory of human nature. We can't help but want more: more diversity, more money, more happiness, more fun!

Up on a pedestal

When we achieved our goal of financial freedom and gave up our jobs we weren't exactly Mr and Mrs Trump but we were doing pretty well. Our lifestyle continues to improve because we have had the time to be proactive and creative in our approach to investing. Had we stayed in our jobs we may not have had the space and time to think as expansively.

Quitting our jobs attracted the attention of other investors and we were invited to speak at a Sydney investor meeting. The organiser was a lady I refer to as *The Investor*, and there is more about her in the following chapter. She was eager to put us up on a pedestal because we had given up our day jobs to live solely off our property portfolio. "*You are,*" she told us, "*where all of these people want to be. They are excited and inspired by what you have achieved and they want to hear what you have to say.*"

Being in the limelight was fun but I wanted others to join me in the ranks of the financially free. I remember asking the audience, "*If you really want to quit your job and get out of the rat race, imagine what you'll do when you're out? How will you spend your time? How will your life be better? How will it be different?*"

As I accepted an enormous bunch of flowers and the audience applauded enthusiastically I felt a strange mix of emotions wash over me. I felt elation as I was touched by the warmth and jubilation of the crowd but then felt confused and wondered why more people weren't doing what we were doing. Although Simon and I had worked hard to achieve our financial goals, it had been fun. I felt like I was playing a part in a play. I was there because everyone loves heroes.

Seriously important

When you get put up on a pedestal and enough people tell you you're clever, you begin to think it is the truth. With several more speaking engagements and some media exposure under my belt, my confidence levels soared to dizzying new heights.

For years I had wanted to be taken more seriously and to be thought of as clever. Finally my dream had come true. Not only did I feel clever but I felt important too. For a while I wallowed in these new feelings. The trouble is when people begin to take you more seriously there is a danger that you will begin to take yourself too seriously.

Life is a balancing act

The following year Simon and I were so busy being important and clever we forgot our wedding anniversary. We remembered three days afterwards. In between property purchases, renovations and holidays, we had been speaking at investor meetings and conferences. Our lives had become hectic and I was beginning to suspect that being clever and important was a little overrated.

At an investor luncheon a lady had approached us and questioned whether we had really 'left the rat race' because we were still working doing renovations and property management. She wondered why anyone who had achieved financial freedom would bother to continue to work. Simon had told her that we continued to work on our properties because we enjoyed it. A simple enough answer but the lady frowned, seeming dissatisfied with the answer. I wondered what she would do. Did she see herself living on a tropical island sitting by the pool all day sipping cocktails?

I've been to tropical islands, sipped cocktails by the pool, and snorkelled with amazing multi-coloured tropical fish. I've travelled the world shopping and sightseeing and I've probably enjoyed more beach getaways than I've had hot breakfasts. I live a lovely life but I also enjoy spending time with family and friends and they are not all about to up sticks and move to a tropical island with me. Simon and I enjoy doing ordinary things, like walking along our local beach or travelling on a ferry to the city. We also enjoy our property related work because it gives us a sense of satisfaction that endless holidays just can't match.

Life is a balancing act and without a boss to tell us what to do, Simon and I had to find ongoing projects that would stimulate our minds. When things eased off and we had no renovation projects going my pace slid from hectic to calm. While moments of calm are nice, too much down-time is no good either. I didn't feel very clever or important when I felt my life was out of balance.

Queen of the couch

The glow from the fire was peaceful and warming. Knowing it was freezing outside, I lazed comfortably on the couch in the semi darkness watching the flames dancing in the fireplace. My life had become extremely comfortable and I had much to be grateful for. I had a nice home, nice things, a nice car, nice friends, went on lots of nice holidays. But in spite of my very nice life, I couldn't seem to fight the rising feeling of melancholy that was building within me.

My house was too neat and way too quiet. There were no shoes to trip over or dirty socks to collect. No books strewn over the dining room table. The kitchen bench was clear of crumbs and dishes. My kids were growing up and spending less time at home. When they weren't at school they were either playing sport, working in part-time jobs or out with their friends. My role of housewife and mother was changing and I needed to adapt.

When I had quit my nice safe secure job a couple of years earlier, I wanted to spend more time with my family. It seemed they had grown up so quickly. They'd become bigger, busier and more independent, leaving me too much time to laze on the couch. I knew I hadn't become entirely obsolete but it was becoming apparent I needed to go out and **get a life**.

The opportunity to march to my own tune had been a big motivator for me. I liked the idea of calling the shots and doing things my way. The trouble was that my march had slowed down to a saunter. Although I loved it that I didn't have to show up at work five mornings a week any more, I realised I needed to pick up the pace and find some excitement in my life before my comfortable couch swallowed me up.

As I sat watching the fire I remembered the lady, and others like her, who was so keen to know what life was like when you don't have to worry about money and when you have regained control of your time. The reality for me was that life is as exciting as you make it. I appreciated the choices I had available to me and I decided to make some changes. I felt that I was bursting with potential that was underutilised. Being Queen of the Couch was not for me. My life, like some of our properties, was ripe for renovation.

Rousing myself from my royal seat, I strolled over to a pile of papers to find something stimulating to read. I came across a list of courses at a local evening college. The Latin ballroom dancing course leapt off the page at me. This was it. When I excitedly told Simon about it he looked up and smiled. I think he would have agreed to anything to see the melancholy look disappear and be replaced with the enthusiasm and passion he was used to seeing.

Ballroom buddies

Our Latin dance classes proved to be so enjoyable I felt like I had discovered a new addiction. Not only did I love the dancing but I made new friends and delighted in the affection and camaraderie that we developed with our fellow students. I found it both exhilarating and hilarious being picked up and spun around by dance partners whose enthusiasm was infectious. As I danced and giggled my way around the hall, I felt on top of the world.

Dancing with my ballroom buddies gave my spirits a huge boost. I wondered that there wasn't a law against feeling so good.

Taking myself seriously had been as boring as lying on the couch too often. From now on I wanted to enjoy my life and have fun. The Queen of the Couch was becoming the *Queen of Fun*.

The beauty of imbalance

The thought of going dancing a couple of nights a week may not set your mind ablaze, but it enabled me to gather the momentum I needed, by giving me extra mental, physical and social stimulation. It was a step in the right direction and sometimes a little shift is all we need to regain our equilibrium.

I used to think that I should strive for balance all of the time in my life, but now I understand that it is the times when I've been *out of balance* that have provided the best learning curves. How do we appreciate true balance and harmony in our life until we've experienced imbalance and stress? How do we recognise *too busy* until we overload ourselves with commitments? How do we know what *boring* really means until we've had too much time on our hands? How do we appreciate our friends until we've felt lonely?

If you find yourself out of balance, recognise it as an opportunity to change. No matter how wonderful your life is at this point you can't expect to maintain the balance just as it is right now. Things change: yourself, your environment, your family and friends; everything changes. The trick is to be as adaptable and flexible as you can be and enjoy the ride.

As I juggle my continually changing preferences and priorities, I have had to sometimes remind myself to relax and have fun. There have been times when I have taken myself way too seriously. Then I remember how important it is to laugh with friends. When I find plenty of reasons to laugh, balance comes more naturally to me. Laughter feeds an optimistic approach to life that makes it easier to regain your balance once you have digested yet another learning curve.

The fun of running in the race

There may not always be a magic signpost on the side of the road marking the finishing line or saying *Congratulations! You've made it*. Sometimes we can be so absorbed in running the race that we don't realise we've run past the finishing line; so busy enjoying our journey that we don't recognise how much we have achieved.

As I got better at property investing and became excited about my goal, I gathered momentum. It felt great to race along at full speed but every so often I had to allow myself to relax a little. Looking back, I know that the best part of the whole experience was exactly that: the whole experience. Waking up one morning knowing I didn't have to go to work was a wonderful moment and one that I still treasure but the process that got me there is the real reward. If we run in a race just to win, we risk losing sight of how much fun running can be. It is the thrill of the chase that sets our heart racing, not just the glory of winning.

Mixing with highly successful investors brought this message home even more. When I met people who had a lot more money that I did, it was brilliant to observe their enthusiasm for what they did. Yes, they were making money, but they were doing it because it was fun and the stories in the following chapter, *Magnificent Mentors*, further demonstrate this point.

15

Magnificent Mentors

Learning and being inspired by other's brilliance

Who are Magnificent Mentors?

Magnificent Mentors are people who know more than you do on a given subject or subjects and are willing to share their knowledge or expertise. They inspire us to want to become more and provide clues to our own success.

I have had many *Magnificent Mentors* because there was so much I wanted to learn.

To connect with a *Magnificent Mentor* I first needed to be open-minded and willing to admit that I didn't have all the answers. It wasn't that *Magnificent Mentors* had all the answers either. No one does. We are living in a world that is constantly expanding. New questions are being asked every day; new questions that require new answers. *Magnificent Mentors* are people who are getting great results and love what they do. They are confident in their expertise yet acknowledge that they themselves are always learning and encourage others to do the same.

In comparison we find contrast

Simon and I sought out other successful investors who had already acquired a significant property portfolio.

We listened to their stories and compared their strategies and adopted aspects of their strategies that best suited our personalities and investing style. We observed what we considered were these people's greatest strengths and the attributes that set them apart from the crowd.

Not everything we observed were things we agreed with. There were some aspects of the successful investors that were less appealing. That is why I would not limit myself to search for only one mentor. I have sought out mentors for different areas of my life. Some people I admire for their wealth creation strategies. Some I admire because they achieve and maintain a fabulous state of health and fitness. Others I admire because of their personality and their ability to bring out the best in those around them.

Contrast helps us to define our preferences. Some view contrast and become overwhelmed because they are not willing to put in the effort to sort out the good from the bad. Others just want a quick fix. *'If I just copy this person then I will get what they have got'* but in their impatience they fail to realise that if we got all our answers from one source, life would be very boring indeed!

Where do you find mentors?

Many of the books I read recommended looking for mentors; people who are experts in the field you wish to excel in. At first I wondered where on earth I would find mentors. I didn't know what type of person I was looking for, so I didn't know where to begin my search.

From conversations with family, friends and colleagues I began to get some leads. One work colleague introduced me to a friend who also had some investment properties. He in turn recommended us to www.somersoft.com.au, an Australian property investment forum. We found this to be a great way to link up with like-minded others, initially through reading and posting on subjects that interested us, and then by attending events and meetings in our area. Through this we made new friends and found it fun to go to investor meetings where we were able to *talk shop*.

Three Magnificent Mentors

Can you imagine stumbling upon three amazing mentors all in the space of a week? Well, that's what happened to me about five months before Simon and I quit our jobs. We attended two events in a week.

The first was the educational meeting for investors (the one I mentioned in the previous chapter) and it was at this meeting that we met our first mentor whom I shall call *The Advisor*.

The second event was called *the Big BBQ*, organised by a lady I shall refer to as *The Investor*. I had read many of *The Investor's* posts on the forum and was eager to meet her because I saw a depth in her writing that outshone many of the other contributors. It was at *the Big BBQ* that we were to meet both *The Investor* and a third *Magnificent Mentor*, whom I shall call *The Renovator*.

My memories of meeting these three people are still crystal clear. With each one of them, I knew straight away that I had stumbled onto a brilliant mind and that it was up to me to make the most of the opportunity to learn from them.

It is worth noting that when I met these three people, Simon and I had already acquired a significant property portfolio. I have met investors who expect to meet brilliant mentors right from the start. But it is often not until you grow your knowledge and experience that you increase your aptitude to ask pertinent questions and thereby earn the respect of a Magnificent Mentor.

From my own experience, it is much more enjoyable for me to speak with a property investor who has spent time researching and playing the field than to speak with a beginner who wants fast answers and is asking general, open-ended, non-specific questions that expose their lack of understanding. Be patient in your learning and mentors will appear when you begin to ask the right questions.

The Advisor: savvy and financially fearless

When I met *The Advisor* I was thrilled because I had finally found a qualified financial advisor who had more money than I did. He taught Simon and I a great deal about finance, interest rates and world economics. He spent time patiently explaining different ways of utilising equity and expanded my knowledge of the concept of making your money work harder. He challenged us to look at a bigger picture and opened our minds to new possibilities.

The Investor: funny, inspiring and surprising

Have you ever met someone with whom you make such a strong immediate connection that you feel riveted to the spot, drinking in their every word? Well, that's how I felt when I met *The Investor*. I knew straight away that she was going to be a *Magnificent Mentor*. As she told me about some of her investment strategies, I felt a raw, unbridled enthusiasm in her manner. She was like an unpolished gem. She was down to earth in many respects and yet soared far above the crowd with her high ideals and grand plans.

She didn't finish high school but fumbled her way into a fortune at an early age by investing in real estate. Through a series of mistakes, she found herself bankrupt and divorced before the age of 25. She told me that this was a devastating experience. But her resilient nature made her determined to succeed. Within several years, she had more than regained her earlier financial position.

The Investor shared many colourful stories of her journey to financial success. Her stories always had a lesson in them and most of the time they were very funny.

I have included the story below to dispel the notion that successful people are *just lucky* or that they get things right the first time. *The Investor's* stories were invariably of the many mistakes and learning curves she had along her path to becoming a very wealthy woman. *The Investor*'s resilience was reassuring, as was her gutsy, adventurous nature.

Blue lattice

You know what it's like when you're renovating a house and you're working to a deadline. There is so much to do. I was doing a reno on this house in Brisbane. I'd been working inside the house and every time I walked along the hallway this nail kept snagging my tee-shirt. It wasn't that it was a good tee-shirt. It was just getting really annoying but I was so busy I hadn't taken the time to do anything about it.

I'd moved outside to spray paint some lattice. When I came back into the house and along the hall that nail got me again. Damn, I thought, I'll fix this stupid nail. I turned and Wham! I attempted to knock it back into the wall. By the time I realised that I was holding a can of spray paint and that this was not ideal for use as a hammer, it was too late. The lattice outside was a brilliant shade of blue and now, so was I. A tradesman in another room heard the explosion and my scream and came to look. All he could do was laugh. I was not amused at the time but I guess I must have looked pretty funny.

The Investor often shared stories of her experience renovating houses and I loved that she made me laugh out loud, again and again. I could picture her with her wide, bright eyes peering out of her startled face, with her wild red hair now an intense shade of blue. It was stories like these that made *The Investor* such an engaging and entertaining mentor. With a substantial portfolio of residential and commercial property, shares and numerous businesses she was someone worth listening to.

The Investor didn't do anything on a small scale; she was full of big, bold schemes. One day she sat in front of me with pen and paper and created a mind map of a large-scale business plan. I was totally fascinated. I had never before met anyone who dared to think so big. On the subject of money and business, *The Investor* opened my mind in a way no one else had.

Where many people spoke of risk and expressed their fear, *The Investor* saw opportunity and felt excitement. She inspired me to soar to wonderful new places in my imagination, which motivated me to adopt a bolder approach to investing.

The Renovator: reassuring and uplifting

The Big BBQ event all those years ago turned out to be a big bang of excitement for me. Still on a high from meeting *The Investor*, I was in for another treat that day—when I met *The Renovator*. I remember standing listening to him, feeling mesmerised. His voice was soothing and he expressed himself eloquently. He had a way with words and a charismatic charm. He had been investing in property for many years and had a track record of buying property below market value and adding value through renovation.

Of all the property investors Simon and I had met, *The Renovator* had a strategy that was most like ours. He listened to our stories and gave us reassuring feedback and he amazed and inspired us with accounts of his latest schemes and dreams. *The Renovator* was a very wealthy man and I think of him fondly because he gave us his time and shared his wisdom so freely and sincerely.

Clever connections

Everyone we meet has the potential to teach us something. Some teach us about things that we want and others make us (sometimes painfully) aware of what we don't want.

Those who have the strongest positive influence usually do so through their passion and vigour for life. When you are enthusiastic about something, you project an optimistic energy that acts like a magnet to others. *Clever Connections* are people who are on the same wavelength as you, people who feel good to be around. Not all of my mentors have taught me about money or property. The following story is of a man who taught me about leadership.

The four 'F' words

Singing in the church hall was not a regular gig for me but this Saturday evening proved an exception. Les Smith was celebrating his 85th birthday at a party organised by his wife Maureen. Simon and I were honoured that we had been invited to perform at this special event.

It had been my great pleasure to play alto saxophone in the Weston Creek Community Band for over 10 years. During this time Les had conducted the band with immense passion and dedication. He had written scores of arrangements for the band to perform. His musical expertise was brilliant.

Les had welcomed me into the band not long after its inception. He knew I was not an experienced musician but he encouraged me to come along. Soon after I joined, the band was due to play in a competition. I told Les I was not familiar enough with the music and did not feel confident that I would play up to the standard required. With his usual optimism, Les encouraged me to join in. He told me just to play the parts I felt comfortable with. He wanted me to be part of the event. I did go along and was glad because I got to know some of the other band members and we ended up in second place! It was a great experience.

My playing improved over time but I knew there were quite a number of members of the band who were more skilled musically than I was. Reading difficult scores was not a strong point for me. This didn't deter Les from giving me opportunities to play a solo part. When I baulked at the sight of a difficult piece, Les would show up at the next practice with a tape recording of the piece. He knew that I found it much easier to learn the music if I could listen to it as well as read it.

Les held the greatest respect for each and every band member. The band numbers swelled to over 60 when there was a big event coming up. Top musicians from around town would come to play in his band. At concerts, Les would come dressed in his suit and hold his head up high as he raised his baton. He was not a tall man but he would swell up with pride as he stood before his beloved band.

When Les had vision problems in his early eighties his devotion to the band did not waver. He reached a stage where he was unable to see until he had an operation on his eyes. For the several weeks before the operation he spent a lot of time at home. Not one to be idle, he composed a march in his head entitled 'Weston Winds'. He had to wait until after his operation, when he could see again, before he could put the music on paper.

Les enjoyed slipping a little humour into his commentary at concerts. During his speech on his 85th birthday party he began by saying "there are four F words" and then he paused while he gave us time to think about this. "Friends, family, fame and fortune," he declared. He went on to say that although he had not achieved great fame or fortune, he had been blessed with a life enriched by his family and friends. He concluded his brief speech with the question "Who could ask for more?"

Les was a Magnificent Mentor to me because he always offered his encouragement and support. I admired his passion for music and the leadership and dedication he provided to the band.

Due to ill health, Les retired with great reluctance at age 84. Last time I spoke to one of the band members, she told me that the band is now called 'Weston Winds' and that they perform Les's march at either the beginning or end of every concert. Les died in August 2007 but fond memories of him and his music live on in my heart.

The value of peers

For the first 11 years of our marriage, Simon and I lived with our teenage children. They didn't all live with us at once but we have watched the six of them grow and mature into adults. It has been an interesting learning curve and one through which I have greatly valued my friends and peers. Speaking with parents of other teenagers made me realise that parents need just as much support teenagers do: support as we observe our children go through a period of transformation and mature in a world that is forever changing.

The next story is about the value of peers and it belongs in this chapter because I believe that mentors come in many forms. It has sometimes been my peers or friends who have reminded me how to be a good Mum or a wonderful wife or maybe even a better person. Their wisdom and inspiration has contributed a great deal to my happiness, without which money would be no fun.

Tales from the kitchen bench

A group of mothers sat around a kitchen bench pondering the mammoth achievement of raising teenagers and watching them become adults. One mother said, "You're doing alright if they reach 18 and you haven't had to front up at the police station," and the others laughed.

Before long the stories began to flow. The 14-year-old who had been expelled for selling 'herbs' at school, the 15-year-old who 'found' a movie camera at the local mall. He seemed to have developed an uncanny ability for 'finding' things. Then there was the 17-year-old girl who couldn't park for peanuts or back out of the driveway without scraping the car but somehow managed to get her driver's licence.

There were young teenage boys who go through the 'I'm too lazy to enunciate' phase and their main mode of communication becomes a series of grunts and nods. Clever mothers soon find clues to what they are saying from changes in their intonation pattern. There were young teenagers who drank and smoked too much before they were supposed to be allowed to do those things anyway and tales of habitual waggers who only seemed to attend school as a social outlet. But the academic underachievers weren't the only ones mothers worried about. There were also the nerdy over-achievers who excelled at school but had trouble making friends. There were stories of the high school extracurricular junkies who spent crazy hours training, practicing and studying. It was tiring just listening to their weekly schedule.

The mothers recalled hair-raising driving lessons, spectacular sporting injuries, harrowing hospital visits, appointments with school counsellors and a dreaded invitation to the principal's office. One mother said the best advice she had received from a school counsellor was to "be patient" because teenagers are more likely to change their attitude in their own time, not yours.

The mothers had heard it all. Some of the stories might not have been very funny when they happened but now the mothers laughed at friends who didn't have kids and thought their personal problems were a big deal. Having teenagers around helps you to not take yourself too seriously.

One mum told the story of a man she had met at a personal development training day at her work. One session she attended had a *focus on raising teenagers. This man seemed very lost and admitted he had little positive communication with his teenager. It turned out he had little contact with parents of other teenagers, the result being that he had unrealistic expectations of his son. His son had grown up physically but mentally and emotionally he was still very much an adolescent. After speaking with other parents in the group, the father began to realise that teenagers are different. Although they are no longer children, they sometimes lack the emotional maturity to make complex decisions.*

The teenagers being discussed this day were not unusual, nor were their mothers. Colourful accounts of unruly teens are not hard to come by. Teenagers may at times need guidance but they equally need love, encouragement and understanding from adults.

The mothers around the kitchen bench knew this. They loved their teenagers and knew the value of peers. They treasured their friendship for all the support they gave each other as their teenagers grew.

If kitchen benches could talk, oh what tales they could tell!

The concepts of *Lucky Links, Powerful Partnerships, Clever Connections* and *Magnificent Mentors* are simply an expansion of friendship and camaraderie. We thrive when we make the most of our clever friends and encourage them to enjoy the best of what we have to offer. My friends, like me, are not perfect but we appreciate the good things about each other and endeavour to disregard the rest. Sometimes we get mileage out of our imperfections. We see the funny side of our less than brilliant moments and marvel at each other's resilience.

> A friend is someone who knows all about you, but likes you anyway.

Who's doing better than you?

We are more likely to find *Clever Connections* and *Magnificent Mentors* when we notice people who are doing better than us. If you want a more abundant lifestyle, look for clues from someone who is doing better than you financially. If you want to lose weight and get in better shape, look for clues from someone who is slim, fit and healthy. Make sure your *Magnificent Mentors* are good role models. There's not much point in talking to your fat neighbour about losing weight. Talk to someone who's got a good track record.

People who pretend they are doing better than they really are often miss opportunities to appreciate the brilliance in others. Look to those whose lives are going well more of the time and follow winners not losers. Choose *Magnificent Mentors* because you like the results they are getting in their life. When you have true conviction and are genuinely committed to making positive changes in your life, people pick up on the energy you exude. *When the pupil is ready the teacher will come.*

The greatest teachers and mentors I've had offer their knowledge, support and guidance, yet allow me to find my own way. They encourage my imperfect attempts and inspire me to live and learn on my terms. They have led me to understand that life experience is the best teacher.

The rules of the money game

Building the confidence to make decisions

Building the confidence to make decisions

"Ten thousand dollars! Are you kidding me? Can you get your money back?"

This was my response when my friend Phil told me that he was planning to attend a course that promised to reveal strategies on property investment and other money-making schemes. Maybe I'm cheap, but I couldn't understand why anyone would pay so much to attend a course that only spanned several days. When it came to education, I wanted the best value for money and I felt that many of the books I had read were worth their weight in gold.

I offered to lend Phil some books, explaining that I didn't believe that he needed to spend that much in order to learn about money and investing. But Phil had already paid and was determined to attend. He *told me he didn't have time to read books and was convinced that the course would help him to learn quickly.*

The next time I saw Phil, I asked him how the course went. He said it was wonderful. He was fired up, as was his wife who had also attended the course. I asked him about what he learned but he seemed reluctant to share any specifics. He told me he had a CD set from the course that he would listen to, when he had the time.

Over the next couple of years, Phil and his wife made several poor investment decisions and they lost hundreds of thousands of dollars. Several years on, they are still struggling to get back in control of their finances.

At the time, I couldn't understand Phil's impatience. I had built the confidence to make my own investment decisions. As well as reading a stack of books, I'd also had taken the time to look at a lot of real estate and talk to agents so I could better assess the market values in my area.

Because I allowed myself more time to learn, my learning curves were gentler and the lessons had longer to *sink in*. The more small decisions I made, the easier it became to make big ones. If I had learned everything really fast, I would have missed the thrill of the chase. My ongoing pursuit of knowledge has added so much pleasure to my journey.

Phil told me he loved real estate but he also had his finger in a number of different pies. His focus was in many places and he was always talking about some new plan or scheme. Maybe I'm boring, but while we built our portfolio my love of real estate bordered on obsession. Although I realised that I did not have to know or do everything myself, I wanted to build enough specialised knowledge, that I recognised and appreciated the expertise of the professionals I engaged. It helped me to ask more intelligent questions which led to more definitive answers. I took the time to understand how I was going to make money from real estate and researched to the point where I felt compelled to act and no longer felt a need to seek the advice of others.

A financial advisor once told me that I shouldn't put all my eggs in one basket but I'm glad I didn't take that advice. There is another expression that goes, *Put all your eggs in one basket and watch it grow.* My point is not whether or not to diversify into different asset classes, but more that you focus enough that you build the confidence to make your own decisions.

Your success is up to you

The car park was dimly lit and dingy, typical of many inner-city, multi-level car parking stations. Our conversation was animated as we made our way to the street and the bright lights of Kings Cross. One of my companions had bought an apartment in an adjacent complex and was deciding whether or not to buy a car space or continue to rent one. Out of interest, I asked her what rent she was paying on the space and how much it would cost to buy it. As a matter of habit, I whipped out my phone and used the calculator to assess the return and wondered aloud what the projected capital growth would be on a car space in the area and pondered how long it would take to get your money back on this type of investment.

Another friend in the group, Belinda, seemed fascinated with my quick appraisal of the two choices. She asked me how I had come to learn about investing and was eager to understand how she could become more financially savvy.

Belinda and her husband are high-income earners who live an affluent lifestyle. Both are university educated and know how to earn money, but Belinda's questions prompted me to ponder the difference in our way of thinking about income. She was used to working for money and I had learned how to have money work for me. At the time, Simon and I were deriving our income solely from our residential property portfolio.

I'm no mathematical genius, nor am I familiar with every type of investing on the planet, but I sometimes forget how much I have learned. I wondered where to begin. Belinda had asked loaded questions and the first thing that came to mind was to tell her about some of the books I had read because I knew she was a prolific reader. With years of university study under her belt, Belinda was open to the idea that financial literacy is something worth investing time in. Unlike others who had previously approached me looking for fast answers and wanting rapid results, Belinda loved learning. She understood that the learning curve itself is where a lot of the fun lies.

But after reading several books, Belinda expressed frustration that her husband was not interested in reading. He was happy to leave the learning to her. Belinda knew that Simon had read many of the books that I had read and that he and I had worked as a team. She wanted to find a way to motivate her husband to learn and work with her so that they could build a stronger financial future together.

Belinda's desire to involve her husband is perfectly understandable, and I have met others who have expressed frustration at their partner's lack of interest. And this prompts me to present the following stories that demonstrate the point that your success is up to you.

Is your spouse an ideal business partner?

John and Libby bought into a franchise and it went well for a while but after a year or so the franchisor approached them with an opportunity to set up another outlet in a nearby location. John was already working long hours and was not keen to take on the extra responsibility. But the franchisor explained that if he chose not to take it up he would be faced with competition and the possibility of losing business to the other outlet.

John chose to take on the additional franchise but unfortunately it didn't work out. The cash flow from the new outlet did not meet the cost of the extra debt they had taken on to set it up. Because they had borrowed out of their home they ended up losing both businesses as well as their home. John and Libby now both work for wages.

From my brief conversation with them I noticed a big difference in each of their attitudes towards the experience. John was much more upbeat. He was sorry they lost their home but he spoke of what he had learned. He could see where he had fallen into the fear trap: 'What if I lose business when the new outlet opens?' He said he had learned a great deal from the experience and he was ready to move on.

Libby, however, was bitter. She blamed John for their demise. She told me that she had not worked in the outlet herself and was not surprised when it all went wrong. Two years after the event, Libby still talks about her misfortune.

John and Libby's story is not exceptional. Here is the story of another couple whose small business failed.

Alan and Connie had reached the edge of a financial cliff and although they did not lose their home, they were deeply in debt. Their home that had been at one stage unencumbered, free from debt, was heavily mortgaged.

Again the difference in their attitudes seemed huge. Connie was more than bitter. She was angry. She blamed both the franchisor and Alan for their problems and she felt extremely hard done by that they had taken such a big step backwards financially. She had avoided working in the business and left the bread-winning to Alan. She had also avoided taking responsibility for the decisions that had been made, even though when Alan had originally thought of the idea she had voiced her enthusiasm for the project.

Alan had gone to great lengths to save their home. He was working long hours in two jobs. Alan, like John, had learned from his mistakes. He was keen to pay down their debt so he could move forward financially. Alan was hopeful, while Connie was stuck feeling sorry for herself.

If you decide to go into a business with your spouse or a family member, make sure they want to work with you. If they are half-hearted they may shrink from the responsibility of making decisions or fail to support you when challenges appear.

A good partnership requires regular discussion, negotiation and joint decision making. Partnerships are more likely to succeed when the parties appreciate each other's attributes, share a similar vision and talk about their financial joint ventures in a positive way.

Enthusiasm is infectious

The look on Lucy's face grabbed my attention. Her eyes were wide with enthusiasm and she exuded an energy that was almost tangible. We were at an investor meeting and before I knew it, I was ensconced in an interaction between Lucy and a girl who had joined our table. The look of confusion on the girl's face was growing and it was becoming clear that she didn't understand the questions, let alone know the answers. She owned two investment properties and Lucy's pertinent questions were exposing big gaps in her limited knowledge of property investment.

Lucy shared a story that first got her inspired about property investing. As Lucy re-told this story I felt exhilarated by her passion and noticed that the girl sitting with us was on the edge of her seat, drinking in her every word.

Lucy, like me, has bought a lot of property. Her strategy is different to mine but equally effective. Lucy has a dynamic energy about her and her enthusiasm is infectious.

This wasn't the first time I'd heard Lucy talk like this but the encounter made me think about where inspiration comes from. It's moments like this, when we hear stories of triumph, see the eagerness on a person's face and feel energised by their excitement.

Inspiration is focused energy that wells up inside us as our imagination expands. It enables belief patterns that may have bound us to the commonplace to be thrown aside, opening us up to the potential of new adventure. When we toil in an absence of inspiration, every action we take seems like hard work whereas any avenue we pursue while in an inspired state is tantalising at every turn.

Free yourself up to thrive on your terms

When you accept that your success is up to you, it frees you up to thrive on your own terms. Lucy's husband does not play a substantial role in their property investing. Lucy described his involvement with the following statement. *'He signs forms when I ask him to'.*

I laughed at this. Her husband is a very creative and intelligent man. He is not interested in property investing but appreciates Lucy's passion and recognises her potential. He trusts her and allows her to get on with doing what she loves and what she is good at.

I am not advocating blind faith here but I am suggesting that you take notice of the potential in the people you are close to and trust your instincts. And, by the same token, rather than expecting your partner to become involved, allow your own enthusiasm to build so that their involvement or lack thereof, doesn't matter.

How much do you need to know to start making money?

When a police car pulled up in front of my house, I thought, "They're on to me, I've made too much money too quickly. They probably think I've done something illegal."

When my friend Lydia told me this story, I laughed. She was relating the story of when she sold her first home and made thousands of dollars in a short space of time. It may not sound like a lot of money now, but 20 years ago, when she was a mere teenager, it had a significant impact on Lydia's life.

Still fairly clueless about the finer points of property investing, Lydia was amazed at how lucrative her first real estate deal turned out to be. Having dropped out of school at age 13, she took a job as a checkout chick, so her formal education had been limited. She worked for a basic wage and survived from week to week, barely making ends meet. At one point she wore a hole in her shoes walking to work. It was weeks before she had the money to replace them.

Lydia had plenty of incentive to want to improve her situation and her story is so good I will continue it. But it is timely that I make an important point that draws all the stories in this chapter to a wonderful crescendo!

The rules of the game

The story of Lydia's first ever house sale provides a wonderful contrast to my earlier story about my friend Belinda who loves learning. Lydia went ahead and made money even though she didn't know very much.

So what are the rules? Do you need to know a lot or can you make money in blissful ignorance? Should you get your partner involved or are you better off going it alone? Should you diversify or focus on one asset class? I could go on and on with story after story of what may appear, at first glance, like contradictions. But this relates back to what I mentioned earlier in Chapter 11: Hidden Potential under the section, *Is it black or is it white?*

Some people are so busy trying to find out HOW to make money. They become obsessed, wanting to know the rules of the game. But the rules are not easy to define because there are so many exceptions and so many grey areas. And this is why there are so many books on the subject.

The answer may seem elusive yet it is really very simple. It is so simple that some wouldn't believe me if I were to present it without these stories. The reason the stories are here is so that you can learn emotionally as well as rationally. If you are only using your brain you will miss out on a big part of the answer.

If you're not quite sure what I'm getting at here, relax. The next part of Lydia's story will provide another clue and there is plenty more material coming that will reinforce this simple truth.

Feel good about money even if you don't have any

As Lydia got to know some of the customers who came to the store where she worked, she asked them questions about how they earned money or made a living. Of all the answers she heard several stood out from the rest. These customers spoke of their success with real estate.

Inspired by their stories she set her sights on saving for a house. She saw her customers as ordinary people and she figured that if they could make money out of real estate, she could do it too.

Lydia's approach was very basic in the beginning. She just wanted to make a profit. But the thing that impressed me about Lydia was that she told me she got excited about money **before** *she had any, because she was inspired by other people's success.*

When I met her she was in her early thirties and controlled a substantial residential and commercial portfolio worth many millions.

It is possible to become energised, enthusiastic and excited about money even if you don't have any. You can get inspiration from listening to or reading about someone else's success. You don't need to have money to get money. You need to feel good about money—feel excited about it—and you can get ideas from observing ways other people make money.

> The trick to money is imagining the fun in having more of it.

It's one thing to get high, but how do you stay up there?

My friend Phil got all fired up when he attended the course and I have seen this happen with others. They find a reason to get excited but the high doesn't last. The momentum slows and they slip back into uncertainty or fear.

I used to find passionately positive people so irritating but then a strange thing happened. My fascination caused me to study them and one day I laughed when I realised that *I had become one of them.* It is not that I am optimistic 100 per cent of the time but I spend a great deal more time being happy and much less time worrying than I used to. And my optimism is not only around the subject of money. It has affected many other aspects of my life. I feel healthier than I have for years, have wonderful relationships and a blossoming bank account.

So how do you maintain an optimistic view of money when you don't have as much as you would like? And how can you improve other areas of your life even when they are a far cry from what you want? Let me share some tactics I have learned that have changed my life.

Emotional buoyancy

Developing faith in yourself

... I have never seen lasting solutions to problems, lasting happiness and success, that came from the outside in.
From *The 7 Habits of Highly Effective People* by Stephen Covey

The only place to put your faith
Confidence is a funny thing. We all have it to some degree but why is it that some people have it in greater quantities? In the last chapter I spoke about building the confidence to make your own decisions but I now want to use a bigger word so that you get what I mean by this in an ongoing sense.

Like me, you've probably known someone like my friend Phil who got all fired up to effect change. It may have been a chunky friend on a new diet; it may have been a lonely friend who has found their ideal date over the internet. Their confidence soars temporarily, but then they hit a hump and fall off their high horse. It all gets *too hard*. The diet doesn't work; the ideal date turns out to have too much baggage; the course they attended that promised to teach them how to make money turns out to be flawed. People face challenges and their resilience crumbles. Their confidence is short-lived because they hang their hopes on external circumstances.

All the enduringly happy and highly successful people I know have a universal quality, and that is faith. But it is not faith in external circumstances because they understand that those are forever shifting and changing. Their faith is in themself. They are dedicated to their own success and trust in their decisions and their instincts. It is not that their decisions always turn out to be perfect but that they are eager to learn and grow. They know that each decision will take them to a new playing field that will facilitate their continuing process of progress.

When I stopped expecting that something or someone outside of myself would give me the power to effect change, it freed me up to build a stronger faith in myself. Now I understand that in order to achieve a significant shift in external circumstances, I first need to adjust my thinking *and* my emotional status in relation to my desire.

I've said this before in different ways but now you may get this more clearly. Are you affecting your world or is the world affecting you? It is easy to get buffeted about by the whims of society and this isn't necessarily a bad thing. Changing fashions and trends keep our world interesting but the only thing that is enduringly satisfying is when I acknowledge that *I* constantly have the power to change *my* world.

Why would you attribute your power to some exterior force when intrinsically you ***know*** that it comes from within? If you truly care what others think of you, make it your mission to impress yourself first. If you are not fundamentally happy with who you are, how can you expect anyone else to be?

We all have the same access

Our personal power is not controlled by some exterior force. We all have equal access to the same positive energy. The only reason some people get better results than others is that they connect with the energy more often and to a greater degree. Some may refer to this energy as *God* but the idea of God can be restricting when people suggest, that because of their religion or dogma, that they have greater access to it. Those who are truly tuned-in to this energy will never expect you to imagine or believe that there is a source of evil. To do this would require that you relinquish some of your personal power.

Everyone has the same access to this energy and it is what drives our emotional responses. Those who understand this will affirm and reinforce your personal power rather than try to convince you that their power is more significant in any way.

When you acknowledge that we are all free to experiment with this energy and express ourselves as we choose, you will feel freer to allow others to tread their own path. Getting caught up worrying about the perceived evil or wrongdoing of others is not a recipe for success. When you relieve yourself of the notion that you should save the world by attempting to control others, you free yourself up to thrive, and it is from this powerful position that you have the greatest potential to positively influence others.

Accessing your personal power

Ways to foster your connection to this source have been alluded to throughout this book and your emotional state is the indicator as to how tuned-in you are. The idea is to feel good, happy, optimistic, excited, enthusiastic and pleased with yourself as often as possible. But could it possibly be this simple? Because so many of us live multi-faceted lives that are laced with intricate details on many subjects, it is easy to lose ourselves in the detail. In the bigger picture, the answer to all that we desire in this life is the same.

We do not progress when we are afraid or uncertain. We cannot blossom or thrive when we are frustrated or angry. We cannot move forward when we are resentful or worried. We have little potential when we feel insecure or guilty. So it makes sense to pursue options that enable you to harness your personal power by attending to your emotional buoyancy. It may be that you feel great about many subjects in your life yet feel a degree of uncertainty in relation to the subject of money. It may be that you want to lose weight or find your perfect mate. No matter what you desire, the answer lies in your ability to access your personal power.

To deliver this message to you in the most powerful way, I again want to engage your emotions. The following stories are designed to lead you to a greater understanding of how you can manoeuvre your mind in order to gain greater access to your personal power.

Good results follow good feelings

Roger was frustrated. The house that he had bought several years earlier had now been vacant for nearly four months, and the last tenants had vacated, owing over six weeks rent. His property manager wasn't returning his calls and the last time he had spoken with someone from the agency, they told him they were looking for a new property manager so there was no one there to help him.

I have met other investors like Roger, who only have one property, so they hand management over to an agency. This in itself is not a bad thing but when a hiccup appears their lack of knowledge can cause their doubts to snowball.

Roger and I were chatting over dinner and I began to realise that my questions were exposing his lack of expertise so I decided to change my tack. I suggested that he focus on the solution: obtaining a quality property manager who would secure great new tenants paying market rent. This made all the difference. Roger's demeanour shifted.

The following morning Roger received a phone call from the agency's newly appointed property manager telling him that he had received an excellent application on the property and was ready to arrange a lease signing.

Some would pass this off as coincidence but those who understand the power of emotional buoyancy know that good things happen when we are in a position to receive them. Those who regularly attend to their emotional buoyancy *get lucky* more often.

The feeling is more important than the trigger

Returning home to Sydney after two years abroad, Mandy began looking for a job. She spent time updating her CV and registered with several agencies. Several weeks passed and her frustration built as she was told that, although her work experience and qualifications were impressive, there was not a lot of work around.

A couple of months later, Mandy had managed to score a couple of temporary assignments but she was now starting to get worried. One day I met her for a coffee and she expressed her concerns. "Is the job market really this slow? Am I being too fussy? Should I just take the next thing that comes along?"

After offering words of encouragement, I left Mandy but she still had a frown on her face. Not having found a full-time job was really bothering her. She normally is a pretty upbeat type of person but admitted she was spending too much time worrying about it.

Several days after this, I received a phone call from Mandy. She was effervescent as she eagerly told me her news. Her boyfriend of several years had proposed to her over a romantic dinner and the following morning one of the agencies she had registered with had phoned with a job prospect that sounded ideal. After several interviews, Mandy was offered the job. She is now happily earning again and excitedly planning her wedding.

Have you noticed that good things happen when you're happy? When Mandy's boyfriend proposed, she was completely surprised. It made her so happy she temporarily forgot to worry about not having a job and in her state of improved emotional buoyancy she was in a position to attract more good results.

Worrying doesn't solve problems. Sometimes problems get solved when we become distracted from our pessimism and become optimistic or happy in regard to a different subject of focus. When you take the time to notice this correlation, you will come to a greater understanding of the value in tending to your emotional buoyancy. Rather than having to wait for something else to occur for you to get relief from your worry, find an excuse to feel happy.

While it is better to focus on a solution rather than worry about a problem, here is another tactic you can employ. If you are feeling overwhelmed by a problem, step back from it. Distract yourself by focusing on some other subject, something that makes you happy. It may be a person, place or pastime. The trigger is not important. What *is* important are the feelings it generates. Spend as much time as you can every day looking for reasons to feel good and see what happens.

18

Manoeuvrability of the mind

Directing your thoughts along a positive stream

Are you putting out the fire or adding more fuel to it?
Nothing makes me madder than listening to people who complain. I really hate it when people whinge about things they don't like and they go on and on. It's like hearing a broken record. They complain about everything from the weather, their poor state of health and how they are so hard done by. They notice all the things that are wrong in the world and find fault with many aspects of their personal life. Why can't they just lighten up and get happy?

There's probably only one thing worse than hearing someone complain, and that's hearing someone else complaining about their complaining. Sure it can provide a little light relief to make fun of something you don't like, but if it goes on too long you add more power to it.

Fuel your desires rather than fan the flames of your fury

Have you ever considered the power of your pet hates? Before I understood *manoeuvrability of the mind,* there were times when I gave too much attention to things I did not want; things that irritated or annoyed me.

Do you know what I hate? I can't stand it when people are too ignorant to see what is right before their eyes. It frustrates me when people don't use their common sense. I mean, the answer can be so obvious but they don't get it. You can try to tell them but they are either not listening or don't even know that they are ignorant! I really hate that!

And I hate it when people don't communicate properly. I really hate it when people don't listen to me. I hate being misunderstood. And I hate it when people misunderstand each other because they aren't listening to each other. It's even worse when whole countries are involved. That's why wars break out.

I used to assume that common sense was common, and became frustrated if others didn't understand something that I considered obvious. I got annoyed when people failed to communicate effectively. But my frustration wasn't helping anyone, let alone me. I knew there had to be a better alternative.

Seek your own truth and allow others to find theirs

When I was new to Canberra, a woman befriended me through a mutual acquaintance. At first I was delighted, thinking that my charming personality had won her over. I soon discovered she was recruiting for her multi-level marketing team. After attending a meeting for distributors, I decided it was not for me.

Years later I was invited to a function run by the same company operating under a different name. I found the speaker's material misleading. He misrepresented another asset class in order to promote 'the business'. The asset class he chose was residential real estate and

I approached him after the meeting to question his data. He declined to discuss specifics and told me that the vast majority of people in his audiences wouldn't know the difference anyway. I felt concern for all the people who would believe every word he said because he was wearing a suit and using a microphone.

Experiences like this have caused me considerable angst. But getting angry about the actions of others was not productive. It wasn't until I began to turn these *pet hates* around in my head that I began to see their usefulness. My *pet hates* or frustrations were a way for me to establish more clearly what I really wanted and when I shifted my focus toward that, I began to feel relief. Instead of being frustrated by ignorance, I realised that it felt good to share my knowledge with those who were ready to receive the messages. Instead of getting angry about misunderstandings, I realised how good it felt to improve my own communication skills. I became determined to seek and speak my own truth.

To judge another's ethics or agenda I would have to get inside their head. I knew that I couldn't control the quality of information that others provided. But what I could do was endeavour to inspire and encourage others to listen to more than one voice.

At the beginning of a financial learning curve, knowing who and what to believe can be confusing. I heard conflicting views on many subjects as I listened to colourful spruikers sing the praises of various methods of money making, including property, shares, franchises, business opportunities, investment funds and multi-level marketing.

There are many people out there promoting their products and services and some people will pretend they know more than they do on a given subject. I always question whether their advice is based on their personal experience.

To determine the quality of the information that was presented to me, I did further research and built on my specialised knowledge. If you want to understand any subject well, scrutinise as much material from as many different sources as you need to gain clarity. Only you can know when you get that clarity and it is an ongoing process. We never stop learning and we never know *it all* because there are new ideas about money every second.

There are plenty of good opportunities out there and sometimes you need to assess a collection of 'opportunities' before you find one that ***feels*** right for you. Glean information from more than one source to find the answers you seek. When you hear different voices singing similar songs then you will know you are on the right track.

Magnetic pulling power

Next time you are feeling frustrated or angry about something, consider the power you could evoke to effect positive change if you shift your focus on to what you want (away from what you don't want). Consider the thing that irritates you as a source of fuel that will motivate you to manoeuvre your mind towards the opposite.

For example, when I have found myself in the company of someone who complains a lot and is pessimistic, I consider how wonderful it is to spend time with people who are upbeat and enthusiastic, and I strengthen my resolve to seek out the company of people who are happy and fun to be around.

Allow the adversity and diversity in your life to prompt positive change. The variety of our life presents undesirable as well as desirable options. *Manoeuvrability of the mind* is about noticing the undesirable options just long enough to establish what is more desirable and then focusing your attention on that desire until you feel drawn towards it like a magnet.

Leave your excess baggage behind

Why is it that some people overcome adversity more quickly and more completely than others? Many people seem to have a measuring stick for adversity. Some assume that the more hardship a person has endured, the longer it will take them to recover, but I have a different view. There are two ways to deal with adversity. Some continue to talk about it, qualify and quantify it, and will tell their story to anyone who'll listen. They carry around their emotional baggage as if it is something they are reluctant to part with.

The second way of dealing with hardship or tough times is to stop giving your attention to it and begin to tell a new story. Some of the most inspiring and amazing people I have met have overcome great adversity in their life and they did it by manoeuvring their mind away from their hardship and the things they didn't want, and re-focusing their attention on what they did want. They found the courage to stop going over what went wrong and started telling a different story, one of an improved, more *perfect world*. They adapted their story to how they wanted their life to be, leaving their old, unwanted, excess emotional baggage behind.

What lights your fire?

Why not put your *pet hates* or aversions to good use by looking for the opposite or whatever you perceive would be a more desirable outcome. The object of this exercise is not to measure hardship or to regurgitate your gripes but rather to help you to discover the power of refined focus. The *Launching Pad* exercise in Chapter 10 is akin to this but now I want to take it further. I want you to discover what really lights your fire because this is where your real power lies. What makes you mad? What do you want to change?

I don't like being told what to do. I hate the feeling that I'm being controlled.

Are you getting a sense now of why I wanted to become financially free? I no longer wanted to work for someone else and I wanted to control my time and my income.

The reason we want more

Why do you want more money? There is one reason why we want more of anything, and that is because we imagine the attainment of it will make us feel better, happier or more fulfilled in some way. And here is something that I really want you to consider. Are you enjoying the pursuit? Is the journey fun or hard work?

In the pursuit of happiness, seek to find it (happiness) all the time along the way. Manoeuvrability of the mind is not just about achieving goals, it's about feeling good and it is *because* you feel good that you will achieve your goals. Sometimes we are so intent on winning, we forget to enjoy the game. We can become so focused on getting to our destination; we forget to enjoy our journey. Embrace your journeys, soaking in every bit of fun along the way.

When you understand that the attainment of a desire or the achieving of a goal is just another step in your life adventures, you will realise how important it is to enjoy yourself while you are travelling to it. This is why it is worth attending to your emotional buoyancy. The pursuit of our dreams is not meant to be a chore. Why not enjoy the thrill of the chase?

Journey to the centre of your mind

A highly intellectual friend once teased me because of my tendency to live in *my own little world*. He was fascinated by my ability to wander along a street in a dream not noticing things that he found obvious or significant. He admitted that he found my evasive nature frustrating at times and I think it was because he was so busy observing what he perceived as *reality*. He couldn't understand how I managed to skip through life, predominantly looking for things that I liked.

One of my psychologist friends has found it amusing to observe me in a group and watch my eyes glaze over when someone is offloading specific aspects of something that fails to warrant my continued attention. Before I understood the importance of being guided by my feelings rather than other people's thoughts, I believed that this was a weakness. But now I have come to embrace my ability to only pay attention to detail when something holds my interest.

The wonderful thing about this is that it frees me up to indulge in my own imaginings: an exercise I now fondly refer to as a *journey to the centre of my mind*. It is a fabulous place where I can disregard the assumptions and opinions of others and of society in general. It is a place where I learned the value of only looking for things that I wanted. It is a place where I realised that the only way to help anyone that I perceived to be worse off than me, was to look upon their situation with optimism because anything less than that would not serve them. When I *journey to the centre of my mind* I see things the way I want them to be. Until I can see it, I can't be it.

Money and happiness in harmony

Watching movies as a kid where the characters lived the high life used to fill my boots with excitement. I imagined how much fun it would be to have endless streams of money available to me. I relished the thought of travelling in style, at the slightest whim. I saw myself dressed to the nines, strutting along magnificent and exotic locations, rubbing shoulders with the rich and famous, because I had become one of them.

These imaginings may seem extremely indulgent but it thrills me beyond words that I'm now in a much more powerful position to inspire and influence others. I dreamed that it was possible to enjoy money and happiness in harmony. And I achieved this by becoming brave enough to ignore what others thought I *should* be doing or *should* be thinking, and paying attention to things that held meaning for me.

Look for good news or make your own

In order to feel comfortable having plenty of money I had to unlearn some things. I had made assumptions that were based on the opinions of others. Wealthy people are not always portrayed in a positive light and society is laced with negative and misleading messages about money. I was led to believe that wanting things was bad, but I now understand that it is our desires that draw energy through us.

We regularly hear bad news on many topics, including money and economic affairs. And the opinions of others often come in the guise of information and this can lead to confusion. I felt liberated when I realised that many wealthy people make money under any conditions. Rather than shrink from bad news they make their own news. When it comes to money, what is bad news to one can be good news to another.

If you look for bad news you'll find it and if you look for good news you'll find it. It all depends what you're looking at and how you choose to perceive it. If you care about how you feel, look for good news. Try taking a *journey to the centre of your mind* and create your own version of good news.

Manoeuvre your mind towards something specific

Have you ever considered the difference between specific and non-specific goals? Have you ever heard someone say 'I would just like to have more money' or 'I want to lose weight'? These desires are general and a bit wishy-washy. There's no wind in their sails.

If you really want to tap in on your personal power, focus on a target that motivates you. The way to do this is to add specifics and here is an exercise that can help.

Begin with a paper and pen and some time alone. It is good to allow approximately 15 to 20 minutes when you can sit comfortably and quietly. The first thing to do is to establish exactly what you want. Use *The Launching Pad* exercise in Chapter 10 or think about your pet hates. What lights your fire? What do you want to change?

It may feel better for you to picture your *Perfect World,* beginning by appreciating the things that you already love, and adding some extra things that would make it more perfect.

Once you have established your general desire, write it down and place a circle around it or highlight it in some way, as this is the focal point of your exercise.

The second stage of the exercise is the fun part. This is your supporting material. Write a list of reasons why your life will be better as you progress towards your goal. Aim to write statements that feel good and support your desire without overwhelming you because they are too far-fetched. Write things that are conceivable to you. They don't need to be earth-shattering but it is good if they are progressive. The object of the exercise is to add specifics that make the goal more real, more defined, more tangible and more exciting.

Focus on the benefits that will come as a result of your evolution. Appreciate that you are not starting from square one. What do you already know that will help you begin?

Use the concepts in this book to bolster you along. Think about how you can relate your situation to the material that has been presented in each chapter. Ask yourself questions that conjure pictures—*until you can see it, you won't be it.* Conjure pictures of where you are heading so that you can add specifics that will enhance the pulling power of your desires. Continue to practice manoeuvring your mind towards things that you want; things that will fuel your personal power; things that will help you to maintain your emotional buoyancy.

Manoeuvre your mind towards your own potential

When you grow your faith in yourself, you will become much less concerned about external circumstances. I came to **know** that I would succeed. I knew that it was futile to worry about what anyone else was thinking, because I had no control over that but *I could control what I was thinking*. That is why I promote the potential of your personal power. There are not words big enough to describe it. With a clear vision of what is wanted, it is easier to stay focused. And when you tap in to your personal power by tending to your emotional buoyancy, and maintain your focus on your vision by manoeuvring your mind, you will feel the magnetic pulling power of it kick in until you become so passionate you will feel compelled to succeed.

> *Manoeuvrability of the mind is about exercising your freedom to focus your thoughts so that you tend to your emotional buoyancy, thereby maximising your personal power.*

The X factor of human achievement

The mysterious part of us

Tracey and Karen were identical twins living in Australia. Soon after Tracey became pregnant with her first child, Karen moved to England. Several days before Tracey was due to have her baby, Karen experienced labour pains. Karen said she knew, even before the first twinge, that her sister had gone into labour. Karen herself was not pregnant and had no children, so this was a unique experience. She couldn't explain how she knew, but said she just knew.

It turned out Karen was right. Tracey had gone into labour early and encountered an almost painless birth, while Karen, who was living on the other side of the planet, had strong contractions.

As a society, we pay enormous heed to our thoughts and deeds. We are encouraged to access information and work hard, yet do not always acknowledge the incredible, and sometimes mysterious, potential of the invisible, intangible part of ourselves; the part of us that feels emotion and sometimes **_knows_** things that our brain has no logical explanation for.

The freedom to focus

Rather than looking for a source of knowledge that is infallible, develop self-confidence and make decisions freely. Worry less about mistakes and instead appreciate the diversity of choice that is available to you. Your vision, knowledge and perception are uniquely your own. Only you can know what is best for you.

We don't all see answers in the same places. In order to thrive, be guided more by your feelings and less by your beliefs. Trust in your own preferences as they reflect who you truly are in essence. Be inspired by other successful people but to become truly happy you will need to make your own decisions and travel your own road.

The rules of the game of life change constantly and everyone's rules are different anyway. Be less concerned about the thoughts and actions of others and more concerned with what feels right for you. When you build on the faith you have in yourself, you will not be looking for someone to hold your hand. Share ideas with others but remember: **your real freedom lies in your ability to focus your thoughts and be guided by your feelings**.

The passion comes from the player not the instrument

A hint of distant music breezed past my ears, teasing my sensibility like whispers in the wind. I walked along the beach toward the melodic sounds until I reached a man sitting on a park bench playing an old guitar. He smiled as I sat next to him but initially we did not speak. I sat in silence, drinking in his music and gazing at the magnificent beach setting that I now call home.

Others had gathered to listen to the music. Little children stopped and stared wide-eyed. Some danced and their parents smiled. I felt so good just sitting there. Time seemed inconsequential as I sat and basked in the perfection of my surroundings.

When we spoke, the man told me that people wanted to give him money. But he was not there to busk. He was playing for the joy of it. He loved the interactions he had with people passing by. Some wanted to talk, while others sat in silence and listened, as I did.

The man had discovered the old guitar in a second-hand shop. It wasn't that he couldn't afford a new one, but more that he loved finding bargains and the old guitar had a distinctive timbre. It brought to mind a friend who had recently paid a lot of money for a fancy new guitar. His instrument was impressive but his playing was not. The man on the bench had been playing for 40 years and he made harmonic sounds that made me melt. He exuded passion with every note.

How do you feel about what you are doing?

When budding investors ask me, *What should I buy? Where should I invest? What should I do?* I feel they are missing something. *What they buy* or *what they do* is not as important as **how they are feeling about what they are doing**. When you are embarking on a new venture, a new job or a new investment consider why you want it. Ask yourself, *How do I feel about this?*

Investing in real estate was an obvious choice for me because I love looking at houses and assessing their potential and I love dealing with people. It was easy for me to become passionate about what I was doing.

When you become excited and enthusiastic about the road ahead your uncertainty dissipates.

Your emotional stance affects your outcomes. If your current financial situation is less than desirable find something to appreciate, no matter how small it may be. Big changes often begin with little steps or small shifts. Use every opportunity you can to improve your emotional buoyancy so that you *feel* better about your financial future. The way you *feel* has everything to do with the results you are getting in your life. This principle is true on every subject. Money is the same.

I know that when I pay close attention to my strategic thinking and am passionate and enthusiastic about my vision, my actions follow naturally and harmoniously. The man on the bench understood this, and his appreciation of the concept of harmony is demonstrated in the following words.

Harmony

We are thinkers and our thoughts create a momentum that carries us forward. Because we can't escape thinking, we can't escape that momentum.

Harmony is the key, and I'm not referring to balance. Musicians are a group who can appreciate that harmony is something that happens along the way and is not something that is sustainable without it becoming repetitive and boring. When we interact with each other it is like a concerto of adventure into the energies around the words we create on the pages of each individual life's story … sometimes the music is flowing and other times turbulent, needing some kind of resolve. Sometimes the music of these interactions is light and fluffy and at other times the contrast is different again.

Harmony is created to be interpreted and expanded upon! Harmony would have no value if there was no contrast or dissonance. Harmony is created to strengthen the quality of the vibe so that the music has more power, more frequencies dancing with each other, so that it can be heard and responded to.

An excerpt from the writings of *The Man on the Bench*.

A chorus of hope

Some people look at our world and see terrible things. They look at suffering and hardship and say they *we* should do something to fix it. But if, in their attention to that perceived or real harsh reality, they become frustrated or angry, they lessen their ability to have a positive effect on anyone or anything.

When you appreciate how precious your emotive state is to your overall wellbeing, you will understand that the best thing *we* can do as a collective consciousness is to look upon our world with optimism and appreciation. Have appreciation for the things, people and situations that are already good, wonderful and often amazing! And optimism for the improvements that we would like to foster, for it is our attention to the positive aspects of our world that give us the emotional buoyancy and imaginative scope to improve what we have and create even more astonishing and wonderful elements to add into the mix.

Our expansive spirit

Hard work does not guarantee success, just as a relaxed approach is not an assurance of failure. Some of my investor friends get amazing results with seemingly little effort. It could be argued that they have already done the hard yards in setting themselves up or doing the research but my observation of people reveals that the results we get do not always equal a particular amount of physical or mental effort.

There is an X factor, an ingredient of human achievement, that is intangible and immeasurable but we know it exists because there is evidence of it all around us. It gets written and sung about every day around the planet. It is the part of us that loves and gets enthusiastic; the part of us that strives for achievement and recognition; the part of us that laughs and appreciates; the part of us that feels passion and elation; the part of us that we can't exactly put a finger on and scientists can't measure.

It is the part of us that has the most potential because there is no limit to what it can achieve when it disengages from our reasoning or analytical mind and instead utilises our creative mind without limitation. What I refer to as *our expansive spirit* is the part of us that comes alive as we embrace the contrast that our desires unleash. It comes from the place where harmony is designed.

In this spirited state, with our imagination flourishing and our enthusiasm at full throttle, we can achieve more in a day than hard work alone will achieve in a lifetime.

*Fun*ancial freedom

Making the most of your multi-faceted mind

Thinking *and* feeling your way to success

Our minds are so wonderfully active and responsive. My mind takes me to amazing places and I am often fascinated at how easily it wanders. Maybe that's why I didn't make a good student. My thoughts can go off on a tangent in the blink of an eye. But now I know that this is not necessarily a bad thing. It keeps my life interesting.

Sometimes I've felt like I've been pulled in two directions. One has more to do with my external world and is based in logic and reality. The other is more internal and is based on my emotions and my imaginings. For most of my life, it has been my external world, the one based in logic and reality, which seemed to get the most credence from others. Because of this, I was often encouraged to think rationally and rely on facts. But considering only fact and logic felt restricting.

Some personality tests attempt to establish whether you are predominantly a thinker or a feeler. Do you rely more on facts or on your emotions? Do you use logic or feelings to make decisions? There are no right or wrong answers but I wish to draw a distinction between right and left brain tendency. Whichever way you lean, I want to demonstrate how you can think ***and*** feel your way to success.

The logical approach to succeeding or winning at anything is to gather information and experience. But facts are only useful when we make use of them by improving our lives. Information is only relevant when we obtain a benefit from it.

Playing sport is a great example. I have played tennis for most of my life. I've had years of coaching and have learned a great deal playing both social and competition tennis. But winning takes more than just knowledge and experience and there is a way you can think and *feel* your way to success. It is the easiest way to win because it utilises more of your mind. It involves getting into *the zone* where things just fall into place. You know those times when you just land on your feet; you get on a roll and get great results as if some unseen energy is lining things up for you. Sometimes *the zone* is an elusive place, not always easy to reach. But it is worth striving to get there because once you're in it, you can be drawn like a magnet towards fascinating people, interesting places and wonderful experiences.

So how do you get into *the zone*? The secret is to find the fun in what you are doing and enjoy the ***process*** of winning. It's a place where you embrace your mind's wanderings as a way of switching between thoughts and feelings. It happens when you are easy going enough to lighten up and open your mind, while also remaining sharp-witted and responsive. These may sound like opposites but here is an example of how I have managed to be relaxed enough to release tension yet still managed to stay focused and build the excitement that gives me the energy to get great results.

The following are snippets of a conversation I had with myself while I was playing competition tennis. I have placed some of my thoughts in *italics* so you will get a sense of the momentum I built that helped me to win a particularly challenging match.

Use your willpower to change your thinking

I'm standing on the tennis court. The shadows from a flock of birds pass in front of my feet. I look up and watch them fly overhead. The weather is great, sunny and cool, perfect for tennis. I'm feeling good but want to lift my game. We went down 6/4 in the first set. *I get frustrated when I miss shots or make mistakes; when I hit the ball out or play a weak shot.*

I really want to win this match. This pair is good but I know we can beat them. We win another point. *I've got to win, I've got to win.* We lose a point, *too much pressure*. Again I'm feeling frustrated.

I shift my focus. *My partner is great. Easy to get along with and we play well together.* We win a game. My mind meanders again. A lady walks past on another court. *Oh, that's a nice tennis outfit!* Mixed results follow. I'm all over the shop, brilliant one minute, average the next. I shift my focus back on the big picture. *I really want to win.*

Then it dawns on me. *What if I think about winning as a process, rather than an event?* To win the match, the best thing I can do is **enjoy the game one point at a time** and manoeuvre my mind, **one thought at a time**, towards my goal, while maintaining my emotional buoyancy. *Frustration won't get me there. What will shift me into the right frame of mind? I know. What if I focus on how much I love playing this game and how much fun my partner and I have every time we play together?*

I love playing tennis, I love tennis so much. I hit a great shot. We win the point. We win the next point. *This is great. I'm really having fun.* We win three games in a row. We're on a roll.

A ball from another court interrupts our play. I get distracted. We lose some points and win a few; my mind wanders. I chat to a friend on the neighbouring court as I retrieve a ball. More points fly past. *Focus now. We have to win this set. Focus on feeling good. Losing a few points is okay. It makes me hungrier for the win. It's all part of the process of winning. Focus on the fun of this.* We win the second set! *I think I'm onto something here.*

We're into the third set and we're up 4/2. *I'm loving this.* I've hit some great shots that surprise my partner and totally amaze me. *Where did that come from? Wow, I love it when I play like this.* My partner is on fire too, powering away hitting random unreturnable bullets. *Our teamwork is awesome. It's like we are reading each other's minds; anticipating each other's moves.* The game score is 5/2 and the score is 40/love. I realise it's match point. We lose the point. *Did I get too cocky? Oh, who cares, we're so close now. Lighten up and enjoy yourself.* I turn to my partner and smile. We win the point. The third set is ours. *The match is won!*

Little adjustments to your self-talk can make a big difference. And it is easier to win when you concentrate on creating opportunities to excel, rather than focusing on beating the opposition. Make it your goal to pay attention to your thoughts ***and*** your feelings and **use your willpower to change your thinking rather than trying to control your actions**. Think about your life, and aspects of it, as if it were a game. Enjoy playing it and look upon winning as a process rather than an event.

It is easier to create than to compete

Making money is just like playing sport. It is much more fun when you concentrate on creating opportunities to excel, rather than focusing on beating the opposition. When I had a fluctuating attitude towards money I got mixed results and, initially, it didn't occur to me to establish a correlation between my attitude and the results I got. Now I see the evidence of it. I make money *when* my attitude sits in a positive range that shifts from optimism and excitement to appreciation and a sense of accomplishment.

Another reason for my shift in attitude was my growing awareness of how many people react in situations regarding money. My observations revealed that most people think that money is something that they have to compete for. The exceptions to this were people who really understood how to use their imagination. They were the ones who understand that it is easier to create opportunities to *make money* rather than to try and compete with what is perceived as already being in existence.

Some people seem to think that there is a fixed amount of money in the world. But when you look at world economics, fluctuating currencies and changing market sentiments you will begin to see that money is extremely fluid. It changes hands constantly all over the planet.

If you want to *create* money rather than *compete* for it, use your imagination and focus on offering extra value. We all like to receive value when we spend our money so it makes sense to offer this to others. Another thing to focus on is to offer something unique. But this is where I've seen some people get caught up. They believe that they have to offer something unbelievably, incredibly unique in order to achieve success.

I have a different view.

When I aim to offer something of value that is unique in some way, I am not concerned about similar products in the marketplace because what is important is the way I *feel* about what I am offering. If I *feel* great about the unique features or benefits of what I am offering, others pick up on that.

Another important and unique element is my vision. We all have our own unique vision and it's the one thing you can create that no one can mess with (especially when you keep it to yourself while you build confidence and momentum).

Thousands of opportunities to fine-tune your thinking

Life can be so complex; there is a lot to think about. It is no wonder that our thoughts wander off on different tangents. Imagine how many opportunities we have each day to think positive thoughts.

The snippet of my self-talk during a tennis match was a mere glimpse of my mind meanderings over a two-hour period. Can you imagine keeping your mind on track for 14 months or longer?

Can you see yourself constantly coaxing your thoughts towards optimism in regard to any one or multiple aspects of your life? That's what I did to achieve financial freedom.

If you are thinking that this sounds like hard work, you can relax. It is not like you have to become your own *thought police* and scrutinise every thought to decide whether or not it was a good one. There is a much easier way to ensure that more of your thoughts are on the right track.

We are all born with a capacity to feel emotion. Some people express their emotions more than others, but whether or not you express them, or acknowledge their existence, there is no escaping them. Our capacity to feel emotion is one of the most significant things that make us human. Our emotions have a purpose that many people forget, especially as they try to reason and plan their way through life.

> *You can change your world by changing your mind—one thought at a time.*

Our emotions serve as a guide. When our emotional state deteriorates it is because of our thoughts regarding something that we are experiencing, remembering or imagining, and it is not always what is happening that causes problems, but our perception of it.

If you keep thinking the same thoughts you'll keep recreating the same patterns. In order to improve the way you feel, adjust your self-talk accordingly and change the way you are thinking.

Regardless of what you are doing, be aware of how you *feel* about what you are doing. No matter what you are thinking, pay attention to the way you are *feeling* about what you are thinking. Rather than attempting to monitor your thoughts, it is much easier to monitor your emotive responses. Try to catch yourself early, as soon as you sense a lowering of your mood, because the sooner you shift, the easier it is to bring yourself back up.

How you *feel* is a perfect indicator as to where you are heading. Our emotions are a gift we were born with and they provide ideal opportunities to adjust or *fine-tune* our thinking. Use your willpower to change your thinking and change your perception one thought at a time.

Give yourself a huge advantage

Ideas often flow more easily when we are relaxed and not *trying* to think. That's why we have great ideas in the shower and cook up great schemes and new dreams while we're on holiday. Our imagination functions best when it is uninhibited. As children our imagination is naturally active. As adults we develop a tendency of pre-empting what we think is probable or predictable, based on what we perceive as our *reality*.

Beliefs give us a place to hide, an excuse not to go the extra distance, a reason not to think outside the square. Beliefs can place limitations on us and boundaries around our imagination. Although boundaries can be useful when they help us to perceive definition, they should be flexible because of our changing world. When we expand the boundaries of our imagination we avail ourselves of endless possibilities.

The diversity of a person's life experience is what stimulates and feeds an active imagination. More variety leads to more choices, leading us to make more decisions and causes more energy to flow through us. But our creative mind also needs some breathing space and it is all about balance. Without enough variety and stimulation life can become less interesting and we become less motivated. With too much we can get overwhelmed.

A technique that can help you to maintain your equilibrium, especially when used on a daily basis, is to quiet your mind and release yourself from conscious thought. A 15-minute session every day can produce amazing results. It provides peace of mind, clarity of focus and greatly enhances your sense of health and wellbeing.

For best results, sit or lie comfortably in a quiet place. If you are prone to falling asleep easily, sit upright in a hard-backed chair. Focus on slow deep breathing to help both body and mind to relax. Just 15 minutes a day can save you a great deal of time. People who practice this on an ongoing basis find that their stress levels are reduced so much that they become more productive and more time efficient.

Some people refer to this practice as meditation. No matter what you call it, consider the benefits that emptying your mind will bring. When we're relaxed and open-minded we produce our best work. It is a great way to reduce tension and confusion and it gives your imagination some space to expand. It's like you create a vacuum in your head so you can suck in new ideas from the ether. Meditation can give you a **huge** advantage in that it can give your imagination space to blossom.

Playing with money

As a child I remember once being at my grandmother's house when she arrived home from a win on the pokies. She was not a regular gambler but turned up on this particular afternoon with a handbag full of money. It probably didn't amount to much but she laughed as she tipped the contents of her handbag onto the living room floor and my sisters and I scrambled to count up the coins.

As kids, in our innocence and excitement, we find the fun in counting money but as adults we seem to lose the spirit of this. We become so worried about what we are spending we forget to rejoice in the dollars that come to us. We can get so used to our pay going into our bank account we forget to appreciate it fully. We receive bills and sometimes forget to be glad about the value we have received in the services we are paying for. At night it only takes the flick of a switch to flood a room with light. We can pick up our phone and talk with someone we love even if they are far away.

If you take a more light-hearted approach to money, in the same way kids do, by enjoying counting it and playing with it, it is easier to get excited about it even when you are not actually spending any.

More like a sport than a discipline

To increase my comfort zone around the subject of money, I found the *fun* factor by playing money-related games. I played *Monopoly* as a kid and went on to purchase Robert Kiyosaki's board game *Cashflow* when I became interested in investing. I have also enjoyed practicing the money-related processes in the book *Ask and it is Given* by Jerry and Esther Hicks.

By playing money games I got to feel the excitement of observing money flowing in and out. It felt good to practice spending money in a bigger picture ongoing sense. It brought money to life in my mind in positive ways, which gave me a psychological advantage because it helped me to think creatively, as well as strategically, in a fun environment where I perceived little or no risk. As I looked for ways to become more enterprising and prosperous, money became more like a sport than a discipline.

The art of blending fact and fantasy

Buying property in a market when confidence was low was scary at first. A change in government saw people losing their jobs and leaving town. It was a time of uncertainty and some people we spoke to thought it was risky to buy in a falling market. We were going against the herd, buying when others were selling.

*Our research led us to envisage that the market would eventually stabilise and recover but there was also an amount of blind faith involved. We **imagined** that the market would soon recover. So our decision to invest in real estate came from a mix of fact and fantasy.*

Over the next couple of years the government slowly re-boosted the city's workforce through outsourcing. They engaged contractors to take on government projects and this increased the rental demand and eventually pushed house prices above where they had been when we first began our research. Our leap of faith paid off!

*Fun*ancial freedom

Everybody's version of the truth is a little different. If you think that making money is risky then that is your truth. If you believe it is *possible* to have fun *making* money then that can become your truth. Your truth about money has everything to do with what you believe or perceive. If your view is dim your results will match that. When you maintain an optimistic outlook your truth will naturally shift towards more positive outcomes.

The degree to which you are prepared to focus your thoughts on the positive aspects of your life will determine the amount of success you experience. Positive actions flow naturally from positive thoughts and feelings, which in turn will give pleasing results. I achieved *fun*ancial freedom, which means I enjoy money and happiness in harmony, and I did it by regularly fine-tuning my thinking. And it is easier to attain this when you take a lighter view and appreciate, as I do, that life is meant to be fun.

- *Take a more light-hearted approach to money so that you can play with ideas and feel the fun of it* **before** *you take any action.*
- *Aim to get a sense of how making money can become more like a sport than a discipline.*
- *Discover Funancial Freedom by using your willpower to change your thinking rather than trying to control your actions.*

Work can become play when you are passionate about what you are doing and you think of winning as a process rather than an event.

Renovate your life
Managing ongoing personal expansion

Life is like a house

When I observe the transformation that renovation can bring to a property, I think of life as being like a house. We can renovate a house, bring out its best features and make it beautiful. It looks great and we feel good about it, but over time the colours or decorations go out of fashion. The carpet will begin to wear, the curtains will fade and some of the fittings will need updating or replacing.

We can design our life exactly as we want it but sooner or later things will change and we can either take the opportunity to embrace that change and give ourselves a makeover or choose to ignore it until our life gets outdated and stale just like a neglected old house. When I think of my life as being like a house, the concept of continuous self-improvement and expansion makes perfect sense. When we stand still for too long we risk becoming dusty and musty. When we keep updating our habits, skills and attitudes it is easier to flourish and enjoy the thrill of the chase towards the leading edge of the best life has to offer.

You can change your luck

"You'll like this. It's right up your alley." With these words my Dad placed an article he had clipped from a Sydney newspaper into my hands. It was entitled *"Luck's a fortune—and easy to learn"*. The article focused on the results of years of research carried out by English psychologist Dr Richard Wiseman. He conducted experiments on hundreds of people in order to discover why some people are luckier than others.

When I read Wiseman's book, The Luck Factor, *I was thrilled because it confirmed many of the things I had discovered about luck and success. I was inspired to read about unlucky people who improved their luck significantly by copying the habits and attitudes of lucky people.*

Being lucky has everything to do with our attitude towards life and the choices we make. When I observe my luckiest friends, they are the ones who are a little more adventurous and more inclined to be open to new experiences than spend their life regretting that they hadn't tried something. They are the ones who pay attention to their gut feelings and enjoy more serendipity in their life. They are the ones who have great expectations, who appreciate what is already perfect in their world yet are stimulated by contrast and excited by new ideas and desires. They are the ones who build great relationships and take an interest in those around them. They are the optimistic ones, always looking at people and situations in the best possible light.

The reason some people seem to get all the good luck is that they understand that we create our own luck. They know that when you focus on the good things in your life with optimism and appreciation you set yourself up for receiving more of the same rather than operating in default mode where you have to take what life dishes out. The more we find things to feel lucky about, the luckier we become because a positive outlook is one of the things that attracts good fortune.

Sometimes our *luckiest links* are the people closest to us. My Dad knew the article would be of interest to me and it led to further reinforcement that ***you can change your luck!***

Why can't they be more like me?

For years I had wondered why certain members of my family weren't as easy to get along with as I was. They were less ambitious, more set in their ways and some took themselves way too seriously. I noticed that some of my friends had these tendencies too. I hoped that in time they would learn the error of their ways and learn to be more like me.

When I mentioned this at a dinner party one evening, my friends laughed and the conversation turned towards personality profiling. We discussed various methods of assessing or categorising an individual's personality traits and someone recommended a book called Personality Plus *by Florence Littauer.*

When I took the test at the front of the book, my results showed me to be an even mix of Popular Sanguine and Powerful Choleric. The Choleric in me was bold and imperturbable, just like my childhood heroine Mary Poppins, and the Sanguine in me was vivacious and spontaneous, just like the teenager who dyed her hair green and liked to make her own rules. I liked Florence's light-hearted take on the subject and realised that I related to people like her because we had similar personalities.

A light came on in my head when I read about the Perfect Melancholy and Peaceful Phlegmatic. I realised how I had underestimated, under-valued and misunderstood some of my loved ones. The arrogant Choleric in me had thought they would be better off if they became more like me.

Happy to bring my over-inflated opinion of myself back down to size, I revisited the importance of understanding those who have different personality traits and therefore different strengths to mine. It made me consider that everyone is capable of being at least a little of all of these things.

When I became a bookworm and began to research property and developed a system to analyse the property market, a little Perfect Melancholy emerged from within me. These analytical tendencies also came in handy when I devised a property management system for our rentals. Although at times I have found it hard to relate to the sometimes unmotivated Peaceful Phlegmatic type, I cherish moments when the Queen of the Couch re-emerges and helps me to relax and unwind when life gets hectic.

Paper, scissors, rock

As a kid I remember playing the paper, scissors, rock game. A bunch of us would stand together with a fist outstretched and on the count of three we would present our choice to the group. Two fingers represented scissors, a fist represented a rock and a flat hand represented paper. The scissors could cut the paper but would be smashed by a rock. The paper could smother the rock but could be cut by the scissors. The rock could smash the scissors but could be smothered by the paper. Each had its strength and its weakness.

I liken the four personality traits to this. The powerful choleric has the confidence to make big decisions and the strength to lead yet can become domineering or egotistical. The popular sanguine can be charismatic and funny but can lack depth and commitment. The perfect melancholy can be ingenious and methodical but can overanalyse and take life too seriously. The peaceful phlegmatic has the easy going nature that makes them relaxed and pleasant to be around yet they can lack the fire and motivation to get things done.

As kids we play games that involve simple concepts of strength and weakness, of winning and losing. As adults the game gets more complex but the concepts are the same. We possess many personality traits but sometimes it is easier to hide in one more than the others. If you choose to extend yourself and expand your personal power, you can become stronger in all of these areas. You can choose to adopt a different trait or mode in a given situation. You can still favour your natural leanings yet become more confident in your ability to draw on your personal strength and versatility. Rather than focusing on any perceived weaknesses, develop your strengths.

Understanding personality types added to the picture I had of myself and helped me to take a fresh view of some of my loved ones and those around me. Personality profiling is a great place to discover some of our strengths and leanings and from this we can learn from and complement one another. We can then extend ourselves to become more.

Broaden your horizon in order to refine your focus

If achieving huge goals relied upon high academic achievement and hard work, I would have failed miserably. In order to discover what I was good at I tried a lot of different things. I broadened my horizons in order to see a bigger picture. The more I experienced, the more choices I realised were available to me.

When I feel my positivity slip, I reach for relief by shifting my focus. The more I practice paying attention to my emotions, the better I get at fine-tuning my thinking so that whenever I notice negative thoughts or emotions creeping in I put myself back into a positive frame more quickly. Sometimes taking a step back helps me to look at a bigger picture. Sometimes it takes a sideways shift so I can imagine how another person may view my situation. When we broaden our horizons we can gain different perspectives. No matter what you are looking at there are always different viewpoints. For every negative opinion or belief there is always a counter or opposite view.

As we expose our minds and bodies to possibilities rather than probabilities we free up our creative spirit, which leads us to want bigger and better life experiences that in turn expose us to greater choice as we find more things to like and dislike. Having greater choice boosts our self-confidence and versatility as we continue to refine our preferences and define our focus. The more choice we give ourselves, the richer our lives become.

Life presents us with a smorgasbord of choice. The fun part is shifting through the variety so we can decide what it is we really want, what will make us happy, and what choices make us *feel* better.

The beauty of human nature is that this process is ongoing. When we attempt to stand still or resist change, the world continues to change without us. We can claim to be content with our lot but it is human nature to want to continue to *renovate our life* so we can grow in awareness of the endless opportunities that life presents.

- *Embrace change and make more decisions, say yes to more and no to more.*
- *Stretch your mind and be guided by the way you feel.*
- *Continue to look for reasons to feel good, search for things to appreciate, notice the positive aspects of your life and choose thoughts that **feel** better.*

Make your life an adventure

Embracing all that you can be

When two or more people coordinate in a spirit of harmony, and work toward a definite objective, they place themselves in position, through that alliance, to absorb power directly from the great universal storehouse of Infinite Intelligence. This is the greatest of all sources of power. It is the source to which the genius and every great leader turn (whether they may be conscious of the fact or not).

From *Think and Grow Rich* by Napoleon Hill

Meeting of minds

The more we access our personal power, the more likely it is that we will connect with others who are doing the same. Inspired by Napoleon Hill's concept of a Mastermind, I formed an alliance with a group of like-minded associates.

One of the members hosted our first meeting at his spacious home set in bushland on an acreage out of town. We had come together because of our mutual desire to provide personal development training that would positively impact on people's lives. During the meeting, everyone in the room was alive with excitement and enthusiasm. The charge of our collective energy was enormous.

The format of the meeting was simple enough. We selected one person to act as a chairperson and this person would open the meeting and keep track of time. We took turns to give a report on the status of our business or current project and what goals we were hoping to achieve. Open discussion followed where we gave each other feedback, encouragement and ideas for future planning. It was an extremely supportive and stimulating environment.

Following the meeting, we gathered up food and drink and headed downstairs to a place our host and his family fondly refer to as *The Cave Room*.

The Cave Room

As I walked into the Cave Room I felt like I had entered another world. It had a unique and explicit theme. The walls had been rustically rendered to create a cave like appearance. A huge bar dominated one corner and on it stood various ornaments, including a large rat with wickedly exposed teeth standing over a misty cauldron from which an eerie light emanated. Behind the bar, glasses hung from a rack and bottles adorned the shelves. Alongside the bar was a wall festooned with green bottles lit up from behind. The effect was tremendous.

Candles decorated the walls and the light from the fireplace flickered in the half darkness. Skulls, swords and ancient weapons were positioned in strategic places. Cobwebs hung from the rafters along with bats and other creatures of the night. Oversized spiders clung to the walls and skeletal goblets laced the bar and tables.

Loud rhythmic music reverberated through the room and was complemented by the beating of drums by our host and several others. The atmosphere in the Cave Room was hypnotic. We drank wine, sang rowdy songs and laughed loud and long. At one point I looked around the room at my comrades, most looked like they were in a trance, spellbound by the positive vibes that permeated the atmosphere. I made a conscious decision to hold it in my memory so I could relive it later. Extraordinary moments like this are worth revisiting.

The Cave Room was like no other room I had ever seen and following our meeting of minds, it was the perfect place for a blending of souls.

Collective energy

There is boundless personal energy available to each of us. We are hungry for this energy but sometimes we shrink from it because we are scared by its power. Our awareness of this energy comes through our emotions and the way we utilise it affects the outcomes we get in our life. Our thoughts convey energy and thoughts that are emotionally charged gather momentum. The more you tap into this energy, the easier it is to tune into the frequency where your hunches resonate.

We thrive when we feel good about ourselves and we flourish as we exchange ideas and brainstorm with others. When we join with others who are connected to this energy, our collective summoning can be enormously powerful. That is why it feels so good to play in a band or sing in a choir or cheer at a concert or rally among a group of like-minded others. It is why it feels so good to hug someone you love. When we are tapped into this energy we feel our very best and we know there is nowhere else we would want to be in that moment.

Have more extraordinary moments

I felt absorbed in the moment as I drank in the scene before me: the harbour full of ferries and small craft; the sky as it turned pink with the sunset; a big ship lit up as it was leaving the harbour; another docked at the Quay; people doing the Harbour Bridge climb; the city lights glistening across the water as the sky darkened; the buzz from the throngs of people milling around the bar; people bustling home in their business suits while others strolled along the waterfront in their Friday night glitz and glamour. I felt enlivened by the pulsating energy of the place.

These are my reflections from a night at the Opera Bar in Sydney. I had gathered with a group of friends and, when I temporarily removed my focus from them, and directed my attention on the big picture, the positive vibes of the place permeated my psyche in an unexpected way.

Sometimes I've felt so swallowed up in my busy life that I've forgotten to appreciate special moments along the way. I've become so focused on where I'm heading, I forget to enjoy where I am. When I remember to immerse myself in the present and take in my surroundings, I am in a much better position to take pleasure in the collective energy of people and situations around me and enjoy more extraordinary moments.

What is life reflecting back at you?

Our thoughts are the precursors of our life experience. We create self-fulfilling prophecies because our bodies follow our minds. When we allow our thoughts to run on autopilot we get mixed results. Sometimes we focus on things that we don't want instead of things we want. Thinking and talking about *a lack of* money or health or harmony will only produce more of the lack.

A friend once challenged my habit of avoiding negative news coverage. She told me I should get in touch with reality. But I thought: whose reality? How does it help when I am moved to tears watching terrible things reported in the media?

Much as I desire peace and harmony in our world I know that these things are not something you can *give* to another. We can give money to those in need but the money won't last unless the recipients learn how to become prosperous themselves.

Your reality is the only one you have the power to change. As you take charge of your thoughts, you take charge of your life and place yourself in a much stronger position to influence and inspire others to do the same.

Our emotions reflect whether or not we are getting what we want from life. You have produced the results you have in your life from your emotionally charged thoughts. If you don't like some of the results you're getting, change your life by paying attention to the way you are *feeling,* and choose different thought patterns.

Fine-tuning your perfect world

We spend our whole life searching for things that will make us feel better. We are always searching for the next best thing: more happiness, improved health or greater financial stability. We crave adventure, love and companionship and a sense of success or achievement.

Whatever path you are on right now, we all have the same purpose. We all want to feel good. Feeling good about yourself is the most important thing you can achieve because it puts you in the best possible position to be of value to those around you.

As you picture your *Perfect World* imagine yourself becoming more ... happy, affluent, excited, contented, loving, fun, interesting, supportive; more of the things that will lead you to feel good about yourself. Fine-tuning your *Perfect World* is an ongoing process and puts you in a position of power, not over others but over your own outcomes.

Ten things you love about being you

Write a list of 10 things that you love about being you. It may be some of your personality traits or your skills or capabilities; it may be something about the way you look, think or act. As you review and appreciate things you like about yourself you have more to offer the world.

With a view to further enhancing your *Perfect World,* aim to add to your list things that you intend to become. Trust your instincts and feel good about your choices. Enhance the only asset you ever have any real control over. Throughout life there are so many variables but only one constant—YOU!

Let the power from your past launch you into your future

When I was six I didn't know that my imagination was valuable; when I was a teenager it never occurred to me that I would one day look back and treasure my invincibility. When I was a young adult I didn't realise how precious my optimism was but as I matured I began to appreciate those around me and the guidance that came from within me. I learned to observe the contrast in the world and be excited by the opportunity to expand and improve my life rather than being afraid of change or scared by uncertainty. I discovered how to use my imagination to paint a powerful image of things that I wanted.

Look to your past for all the good things you've learned and all the experience you have gained. Who you are right now is not just a summary of your life up to this moment in time. Who you are now is also about who you want to become. Discovering new desires motivates us to spread our wings. Every thought you have has the potential to make you more; every thought has the potential to produce more good results.

A reminder of our potential

The purpose of this book is to remind you of your potential and I have done this by demonstrating how I discovered my own. In my willingness to continue to embrace all that I can be, I have found enormous freedom. In every mistake, I found another clue; with every challenge, I found new answers; with every twist, I discovered greater resilience. With each step I built upon my skills and strengths and continued to discover new ones.

Embracing all that you can be

The best way I could think of to describe what I mean by *embracing all that you can be* was to give the following description of how I see myself. It is written with the intention of stimulating you to write about you, about the traits you now lean on and some that you feel you have the potential to further develop.

One part of me I think of as *Ambitious Julie*. It's the part that motivates me and strives for greatness; it's the part of me that sometimes feels invincible, unstoppable and imperturbable, and loves looking at the big picture. *Ambitious Julie* is optimistic, focused and directive but has been known to get carried away with her own importance.

Then there is *Fun Julie*. This is the part of me that laughs at *Ambitious Julie* when her opinion of herself gets overinflated. *Fun Julie* is down to earth and seeks out the company of others. She loves being around people and easily engages in conversation with friends and strangers alike. She craves love, laughter and good times and often feels like a child at play. She is adaptable, adventurous and irreverent.

But although these two parts are easy for me to call on, I know that I miss out, or become imbalanced, if I do not regularly acknowledge and utilise two other facets of my personality. The third part I refer to as *Peaceful Julie* and this is the part of me who is opposite to *Ambitious Julie* in that she is humble enough to shove her ego in her pocket and allow others to shine. She listens more than she talks and loves to observe and encourage the brilliance in others. She loves to quieten her mind so that she can hear her inner voice and she, similar to childlike *Fun Julie,* loves living in the moment.

The fourth part is *Julie the Genius* and, although *Fun Julie* finds it hilarious that anyone could take their own intelligence so seriously, *Fun Julie* will take a back seat to allow *Julie the Genius* to be a powerful creator. *Julie the Genius* is inquisitive, resourceful and imaginative. This is the part of me that aims for perfection but will settle for excellence.

If you are not yet convinced of the advantage you could gain from cultivating multiple personality facets, let me throw a fifth and final one into the mix. The fifth part is just called *Me* and this is the part that is clever enough to blend the other four parts of my personality into a person that I am becoming increasingly fond of.

When this whole version of *Me* was brave enough to embrace the many facets of the person I wanted to be, without regard to limiting opinions or ideas of others, I began to truly shine, and it is from this platform that I am in the best position to inspire and encourage others to do the same.

You are any or all of these things and more. When you find the courage to embrace all that you can be, and continue to develop and enhance the qualities and traits you desire, then you can mix them together into a person who you will be very happy to live with for the rest of your life. And as you pursue your own potential, others will be drawn to your authenticity.

Make your life an adventure

When I was a little girl I remember wandering through my grandmother's garden feeling like I had entered another world. It was a mysterious place full of paths that led this way and that, through trees, bushes and flowerbeds. Meandering through the foliage sparked my imagination and I felt full of anticipation at what I might find at the next turn.

As I grew, my grandmother's garden became a little less mysterious but I still remember the sense of adventure that it stirred within me. If we explore the same place for too long, it loses its mystery and excitement. We are designed to find new places and experiences that stir our sense of adventure.

As we wander through life we are constantly presented with choices. Sometimes we feel like a child lost in a maze. *Which passageway will I explore? Where will this lead me? What if I turn down this way or divert from the main path?* Imagine approaching your travels through life with anticipation and excitement rather than fear.

Our job is to explore life and have fun. We know this as little children but as we grow we forget. Our job is not to fix others or make *the world* a better place. Our job is to make *our world* a better place. Rediscover the little child within who has a natural ability to get lost in the world of their own imagination.

Think of life as an adventure rather than a journey. A journey is a trip you have to take. An adventure tantalises our imagination at every turn and fills us with excitement and enthusiasm. Where do you see yourself going in your life adventure?

About the author

Early in her second marriage, Julie's motivation to make extra money was stimulated by the fact that she now had a blended family of six children consisting of three under ten and three teenagers. While juggling the unpredictable needs of her ever-changing household, she searched for a way to thrive financially. She knew that to stand out from the crowd she would have to do something different from what the crowd were doing.

Noticing that her new husband was forever tinkering and improving things around the house, it dawned on her that she had married a serial renovator. With two former homes held as rentals, the couple realised that the renovations, coupled with an upturn in the property market, meant their real estate was making them nearly as much money as their wages.

Over the following fourteen month period the couple bought enough investment property to enable them to quit paid employment. Their strategy has involved buying, renovating and holding residential real estate in three states.

After leaving the workforce, Julie took a strong interest in writing and became involved in activities at several writers centres. Although continuing to buy and sell real estate, Julie dedicated much of her free time to writing. Since 2001, she has undertaken numerous speaking engagements and has been featured in several property related publications. She is also currently an active member of two Sydney Toastmaster clubs.

Eclectic, witty and socially adventurous, Julie has a vision to inspire others to enjoy the freedom of living life by design rather than by default. She enjoys playing tennis, dancing and travelling to exotic locations and believes that life is meant to be fun.

Footloose and Financially Free is based on her philosophies and experiences in achieving a lifestyle where money and happiness naturally co-exist.

For more information about the author visit:
www.macmillionaire.com

milli6,000,000**naire**

Acknowledgements

My mind is brimming with appreciation for those who have contributed to the creation of this book. First and foremost being my husband, Simon, who is such a treat in so many ways; thoughtful, creative and easy going. My parents and my children have listened to me talk … a lot, and they all deserve a medal. Just the thought of them makes me smile. I have many other treasured family members and friends who have encouraged me and shared their enthusiasm for life.

On the road to publication I have formed many new associations and worked with numerous editors. To each I offer my heartfelt thanks, with particular mention to: Malcolm Drysdale, who encouraged me in the early stages; Monica Dennison, who has a special gift for reading between the lines; Helen Elward for her skill in project management and design; and Dennis Jones, for taking the time to read my manuscript.

Many significant interactions have created an emotional surge of good feelings that have burst out of me and onto these pages. And as I think of those who have inspired me, I smile. My body plays out what is written on my heart!

www.ingramcontent.com/pod-product-compliance
Lightning Source LLC
Chambersburg PA
CBHW061318040426
42444CB00011B/2699